My *Intuition* Led Me to *Love*

A Memoir

Brigitte Malisa

BALBOA.PRESS

A DIVISION OF HAY HOUSE

Balboa Press books may be ordered through booksellers or by contacting:

Balboa Press
A Division of Hay House
1663 Liberty Drive
Bloomington, IN 47403
www.balboapress.com.au
1 (877) 407-4847

Because of the dynamic nature of the Internet, any web addresses or links contained in this book may have changed since publication and may no longer be valid. The views expressed in this work are solely those of the author and do not necessarily reflect the views of the publisher, and the publisher hereby disclaims any responsibility for them.

The author of this book does not dispense medical advice or prescribe the use of any technique as a form of treatment for physical, emotional, or medical problems without the advice of a physician, either directly or indirectly. The intent of the author is only to offer information of a general nature to help you in your quest for emotional and spiritual well-being. In the event you use any of the information in this book for yourself, which is your constitutional right, the author and the publisher assume no responsibility for your actions.

Any people depicted in stock imagery provided by Thinkstock are models, and such images are being used for illustrative purposes only.
Certain stock imagery © Thinkstock.

Print information available on the last page.

ISBN: 978-1-5043-0592-1 (sc)
ISBN: 978-1-5043-0593-8 (e)

Balboa Press rev. date: 12/11/2020

I wrote this memoir for my beautiful daughter, Ava. She inspires me every single day.

"The light in me sees the light in you"

Affirmation: "I am beautiful just as I am."

Copy the affirmation on the prior page as many times as you wish.

Chapter 1

Finding my path

I was browsing in a bookstore, looking for a new novel to read. She seemed to come out of nowhere, this lady with long, black hair and large eyes. We both reached for the same book. She apologized and said that I could have the book, she would find something else to read. We entered into conversation and I discovered that she was a lot older than me. Her name was Mary. I was studying at high school and I was very stressed about my year 12 exams. There was something I liked about this lady. She had a very caring presence and gave me some great advice to help me relax for my exams. As we said good-bye, she handed me her business card. I briefly looked at it and thought I must not be reading it correctly. Did it say …? I mean, it couldn't really say … Yes, it definitely had the word 'psychic'. I began to take a step backwards from her.

Never in a million years did I expect that this lady was someone that I would not only visit for a reading, but that one day I would be doing a lot of things very similar to her. Not for one minute did I think that I would actually become a psychic and have many people come to me for guidance.

* * *

In my early twenties, I began to realize that I had a beautiful gift. I had visions and feelings about others that were accurate,

1

and was able to use them to help bring peace to these people in their time of need. At the age of twenty-two I was finally able to understand what people meant by the term *the power of the mind.* I had been endlessly reading spiritual and self-healing books to help myself cope with past pain. The books really resonated with me, and I found a deep sense of peace as I saw I could undo most of the pain that I had endured. I had felt hopeless for most of my teenage years, so this new form of thinking and self-healing was my savior. I couldn't believe how rapidly I healed or that I was finally able to have some positive thinking in my life. I began to understand how I could change my self-sabotaging ways.

It took some amazing angels, entering my life in the form of spiritual counselors and healers, to help me find my true strength. They were the souls who would change my life, as they counseled me with their inner wisdom. These women and one particular man were my angels, and their healing love surrounded me whenever I had a session with them. It was my calling to become like them and follow my own path in healing others.

Sometimes when I think about it, it seems strange to me that I ended up with a career as a psychic; however, I don't feel it is a 'strange' occupation, unless someone mentions it to me in this way. I often believe it is similar to being a counselor guiding people to see the light.

* * *

I was extremely insecure about my looks when I was growing up. I felt unattractive and always compared myself to my peers and the models in teen magazines. Often I would look in the mirror, yearning to perfect parts of my body and face that I believed to be completely undesirable. I drove my mother up the wall with my constant complaining about my looks. She would stare at me in complete disbelief, shaking her head at my behavior.

People often told me that I was very attractive, but I couldn't see it. I didn't consider myself to be attractive in any way throughout my high school years, more like a very awkward, gawky teenager. When I reached the age of twenty, I became more comfortable with my appearance and less insecure about it. I still, however, lacked confidence, and was very shy.

Yet during my teens, I constantly wanted perfection in my looks and would not leave the house until I was fully satisfied with the result. This wasn't a healthy thing for me, as I would take ages to get ready, even just to visit the local shopping mall. My hair had to be perfectly groomed and I was very fussy with my fashion sense. My make-up was also something I would put a lot of energy and time into, and I was very tired by the time I finally made my way out the door. It may sound like I was vain, but I was so insecure about myself that I believed if I had the 'perfect appearance' then I would have more confidence with others. I knew deep down how crazy it all seemed and was fully aware of the time I was wasting, but I was determined to look my best, even if I was suffering in silence.

Some of the psychics I saw told me that it was the fact that I was born a Virgo that made me strive for such unrealistic perfection. Virgo is the main sign that desires to be perfect in every way. I'm certain there was a strong aspect of that in me when I was growing up, and that may have contributed to my obsessive behavior. I also believe it had to do with deeper emotions that stemmed from my past.

The fact I worked in retail fashion didn't help the situation. In fact, it amplified my insecurities even more. I put myself under constant pressure to look my absolute best in front of my customers. I was supposed to set an example for the company which I worked, and I wanted to look perfect so that I could sell more clothes. I was very unhappy most of the time and didn't feel like I belonged in these retail fashion stores. There was the one exception, a store called Mazi. I loved wearing their designs while selling the clothes and attending parties with my friends. It was enjoyable working in this very trendy atmosphere. I enjoyed the customer service aspect, however, and would always listen to my intuition to make great sales. I was very popular with the women who came into these fashion stores, as my sixth sense helped me to understand their needs. Of course, I didn't realize this at the time. Back then, I never understood why I could connect with my clients and convince them to purchase many clothing items without really having to try too hard.

Some of the customers were anxious, and I would unconsciously pick up on their moods. I would frequently believe that it was me who was anxious, not the customer I was serving. It was very confusing for me, as I was taking on board the other person's energy and thinking that it was my own. If I had known that I was intuitive and that I was especially susceptible to feeling others' pain, I would have been able to separate the customers' emotions from my own. I could have taken a little step back from the customers and protected myself from their overwhelming emotions. I could even have left them to find their own clothes while I served someone else. I didn't need to take on board their stress and let it affect me and upset my day.

Empaths are generally so sensitive that we feel others' pain too easily. It can be upsetting for us at times, although we need to sense people's emotions so that we can assist them easily through their difficult times. We also have techniques that we use to block out a person's stressful aura. We are wiser these days, so we do not become unhealthy.

* * *

Retail fashion was something that I did not consider doing

for the rest of my life. The urge overcame me to leave the fashion industry because I wanted to heal others. I didn't know how to go about it but believed in my heart that I was meant to help many people in this lifetime. I never would have dreamed that my way of helping people would involve being a psychic, yet was aware that it wouldn't involve being a psychologist or counselor. I didn't feel drawn to study psychology in any way. There was no passion within me for this industry. I couldn't seem to go down that path, no matter how much I tried. It just didn't seem right to me; my intuition was steering me in another direction.

I attended university straight after high school, and felt completely out of place. I knew in my heart that I didn't belong there. I couldn't understand how everyone at the university seemed able to devote all their attention to their studies. Some of them even looked as if they were really enjoying it. This surprised me and amused me, as I was so uncomfortable at the campus. The energy was very cold, and I had no desire whatsoever to study. You might think that I was just some lazy teenager who couldn't be bothered doing any form of work, but this was not the case. I had done very well with my studies at high school and was extremely proud of my achievements.

I simply was not going to need a degree for the direction in which I was heading. From the day I was born, my destiny was always to become a psychic healer. I wasn't destined to become anything else but didn't know it yet, and I was confused about what I should do for a career. Unfortunately, I was still too young to understand what my true life purpose was. It wasn't until later on in my twenties that I would finally find contentment with my work situation.

I recall all the books I had to purchase for my studies at university, and can't seem to forget the sadness each time I entered its hallways. I was so lonely, insecure, and shy. I tended to keep to myself and I liked it that way. I preferred to daydream and escape the campus during breaks. I enjoyed the calming sound of the tram and would often enter bookstores in the city and buy natural healing books, which I would read thoroughly. The entire university reminded me of a jail and I longed to leave and never come back.

I spoke to my parents about my decision to defer my studies for six months and look for a job, just so I could have a break. I recall the day that I handed in my papers to defer—I was so happy. My parents were not pleased with my decision and now that I am older, I can understand why. They were concerned about my future and they also sensed that I would never go back. They were right.

It made sense that I ended up studying to become a Library Technician since I loved novels. I completed the course. I began to work at several library locations and enjoyed every minute of it.

Everyone I worked with was so friendly. My confidence grew. Yet, after about 4 years I become restless. In my heart, I knew it was time to move on.

Affirmation: "I am strong and brave. I can conquer anything."

Copy the affirmation on the prior page as many times as you wish.

CHAPTER 2

The healer within

I worked in retail fashion for a year, then completed a short administration course. One day a fantastic opportunity arose to work at a well-respected company where I had to assist callers with shares. I still have no idea how I ended up in that job, and I was once again completely unhappy. It seemed that many of my colleagues were unsure of the information that we had to give to our clients, and that made me uncomfortable. A lot of them seemed not to care if the data they conveyed over the phone was correct or not, and consequently I was certain that this was not the right place for me. As it happened, I became very unwell with a virus infection. Work allowed me some time off to get better but I knew that I would never return. I disliked the crowded and fast-paced energy of the city and no matter how much I tried, I couldn't see a future with that company.

While I was going through this troublesome time, I was receiving messages from my angels to keep moving forward. All around me, there were strong signs trying to point me in the right direction, telling me I was in the wrong industry. The problem was I couldn't see them and I was unaware that I was constantly being watched over and protected by my angels. Instead, I felt completely alone.

I ended up back in retail, selling fashion—something that was only bearable for a period of three years. I was experiencing problems with my health and I could only handle part-time work. It was very frustrating for me not to be able to work full-time hours, but each time I entered into a full-time position, I became way too run-down. My anxiety levels were high and they were contributing to my migraines and exhaustion.

I had to learn to listen to my body. It was during these times that I had no choice but to trust my own intuition over what others were telling me, and just follow it through. I had many people giving me different opinions about what I should do and how I should live my life. They were all trying to help me but I became frustrated and confused. In the end, it was my decision and my life. In the past when I hadn't listened to my inner wisdom, I'd become run-down and even more unwell. If I went against what my gut instinct was telling me, I would become sick and my life wouldn't go in a healthy direction.

My parents had given up on me, and even friends were beginning to question my motives. They all said that I needed more stability, so why was I leaving all my jobs too quickly?

Was I simply imagining that I deserved more? Why was the feeling within me too strong to ignore, the feeling that told me to move on? Was I just being foolish for believing that I deserved better?

These were certainly difficult years for me with my health and my career. I shed many tears. I needed a clear direction towards the career that best suited me. I was desperate to find my true life purpose, the career I was destined to undertake, the one that I would absolutely love and gain the utmost enjoyment from—not a job that I literally had to drag myself out of bed for and do simply for convenience.

* * *

I was rushed to hospital. My migraines were giving me

incredible pain. My body was dehydrated and weak. I had been popping too many painkillers to try to help the pain subside. They were forming into a slight addiction. These were not your normal headaches. They were extremely painful and could have me sick in bed for days. I needed to lie down in the dark, as I would have blurred vision and my eyes would be sensitive to light. My migraines were frequent and debilitating.

The nurse examined me and placed a drip in my arm to return fluid into my body. Very tired, depressed and frustrated, I didn't like the feel of this hospital and I hated the fact that I had to be there.

The nurses and doctors all looked at me with pity. It was a bit of a blur and a nightmare, but deep down, I knew that I would be okay. All of this would pass and I would be stronger again. The angels whispered to me that I would help people myself one day. Their words gave me strength and even in my darkest moment, they helped me believe that everything would be fine. In the dark, they were my light. In the dark, God and the angels brought me faith to keep going.

When I approached my local doctor about my migraines, he informed me that I should not eat five particular substances, as they were sometimes the triggers for such headaches. These five substances were chocolate, cheese, caffeine, oranges and red wine. Each time I had one of these, they would no doubt cause me to have a migraine. Within a couple of days of consuming the particular substance, I would be in severe pain.

The doctor also informed me that if anyone else in the family experienced migraines, I was more likely to suffer from them, as they can be genetically related. My grandmother and my aunt both had them. I worked hard at healing them and knew that they would not be something that I had to have forever. They were manifesting from deeper issues within that still needed to be resolved. I had to work on clearing these issues on a spiritual level.

The neurologist I had been referred to prescribed me heavy medication to help lessen the pain and frequency of my migraines but I was determined not to have to take this medication forever, as I experienced awful side effects. I recall telling the neurologist that I would eventually be able to come off my medication. He looked at me as if I was foolish for thinking such a thing and said to me that I would have to take them for a very long time and most likely until my dying day.

Two years later, I was off my tablets. That doctor never found out, as I had stopped seeing him by then. I would've liked to approach him for one final session, to tell him that I no longer needed the medication and that my headaches had improved. I wanted to let him know how wrong he had been to foretell that I would take the medication for a long time, and that he should not have made such a negative and dangerous prediction about my health and wellbeing.

If I had not been spiritually aware and had not understood the power of the mind and how you can overcome health issues by clearing up inner issues, then I would still be on the medication today. I could still be taking it and I would have believed that I was doomed to have severe migraines forever, only treated with the use of drugs. I would have believed his inaccurate prediction, simply because I thought that he was a neurologist and he knew what he was talking about. Instead of listening to my inner wisdom and trusting that something wasn't right, I could have easily believed his words and taken the medication for the rest of my life.

Today I continue to see an acupuncturist. I take Chinese herbal remedies and attend regular yoga classes. I can monitor my health through a more natural form of therapy. I still get migraines, but not as frequently as I did back then. I don't experience any nasty side effects that many medications have. I feel revitalized from an acupuncture session, not drained from the sedative result of having popped a pill prescribed by a neurologist. However, many people who suffer from conditions such as bi-polar and severe depression, need to be taking medications prescribed by their medical practitioner. I believe their minds are too sensitive, and as they suffer from a chemical imbalance, they must be very cautious if they plan to only rely on herbal remedies.

* * *

Finally, I received the message from my angels that I had been waiting for. It happened in the most unexpected way. I was casually browsing in a bookstore when something led me to buy a book in the 'self-help' section. When I made my purchase, the sales assistant handed me a free bookmark. This simple bookmark would have a life-changing effect on me. It was the answer to my prayers and it would lead me in the right direction for my soul's journey. The bookmark advertised an angel seminar, to be held in Melbourne at the Convention Centre, and as the lecturer did not travel to Melbourne frequently, I knew that I had to take this rare opportunity to attend. For some reason, I wanted to attend the workshop, rain, hail or shine.

As luck had it, there were still seats available at the seminar and something told me that my angels were making certain that I wouldn't miss out on this opportunity. I had never before been this excited about attending a seminar and doing some intense study. This seminar would turn out to be something which resonated strongly with me, and it would all make perfect sense to me. Unlike my university studies, which I had found extremely difficult to relate to and enjoy, the information at this seminar was so interesting that I absorbed it like a sponge. It helped to open my third-eye chakra immensely. The reason I had been drawn to this workshop was to help improve my abilities as a healer. The fact was, however, that I had never intended to go to the seminar to become a psychic. I hadn't even thought that was a possible option for me. I only wished to attend as I wanted to learn more about healing myself and possibly healing others.

The three-day seminar was an amazing experience. I was finally able to see exactly the way in which I was to assist others. It had never occurred to me that I would be able to work as a psychic and see things for others, to help give them direction in their personal lives. I was able to combine my healing studies with my intuitive abilities and do what I loved. I was able to begin my own business as an Angel Intuitive.

Basically, the seminar helped to give me the tools that I needed in order to work as an Intuitive and an angel healer. I already had the gift of sensing things and feeling things about others; however, through this seminar, I learnt how to expand my abilities even further, so that I could heal others in this day and age. I was able to work on advancing my intuitive gifts to an even higher level and understand how to use them to the best of my ability. The lecturer was highly psychic herself and travelled extensively around the world to run these seminars, in order to help people like me use their gifts more wisely. Of course, not everyone who attended was going to walk out of there desiring to become an Intuitive healer. Many wanted to expand their intuition solely for their own purposes, and some were just curious about angels and wanted to learn more about them.

My jobs in the retail industry became things of the past. I would never again have to be concerned about where my career path was headed. My life finally seemed to have more purpose. I was extremely grateful, as my angels were always guiding me to my true path. They never left my side. I truly felt blessed.

* * *

When I first began working as an Intuitive, I did many readings for people in markets and shopping malls. Many people wanted to have quick, affordable readings, just for fun or purely out of curiosity. I used to do the markets on my own and I would set up an area for myself. I was inundated, mainly with women who wanted their fortunes told. It was a way of promoting myself and of gaining potential clients. Most of the people who had a ten-minute reading at the markets would take my business card and arrange to see me for a private, hour-long session.

Originally, I loved being at the markets, and I was always excited to go and work there. Everyone seemed very happy with my short readings and my accuracy. However, the atmosphere was so busy and crowded that I would often be overwhelmed with the energy. Soon after, I was asked to join a small group of psychics. We did readings in shopping centers. We were swamped with people and it was very draining. I was already experiencing personal difficulties in my life, and helping so many people was just too much for my mind to handle. I put a stop to doing those readings and I was frustrated, as once again, I had taken on more than I could handle.

One blessing which came from the markets and shopping malls was that my accuracy in my readings improved due to the constant demand for them. I began to only do private sessions at two natural healing centers. I preferred doing the readings at those centers because the privacy and quiet environment made it easier for me to concentrate. At the markets, some of the women were very demanding and would try to stretch out their time with me. The environment wasn't very professional, so I began to attend markets less frequently. Working at the healing centers, my energy levels returned and I relaxed more. The pressure from the markets and shopping malls left my life, and I really began to love my work. Finally, things were starting to fall into place.

Affirmation: "I am wise and lovable. I create beautiful memories."

Copy the affirmation on the prior page as many times as you wish.

CHAPTER 3

My first love

Growing up, my brother jokingly nicknamed me 'Hippie' and said that I should go and live in a caravan and smoke dope, as that would suit me perfectly. Apparently, to him, since I meditated so much and was a very spiritual girl, I might as well go live a hippie lifestyle.

Years ago in her own little village in Italy, my great-grandmother did the same kind of work as I do now and is often around me in spirit. My deceased grandfather, who I absolutely loved and adored, was not very surprised when I told him that I was working as a psychic. He told me that his own mother had many women come to see her for help, and she was known for her tremendous accuracy. Commonly psychic gifts can be passed on from generation to generation; however, I was still surprised by this information, as I had absolutely no idea that someone else in the family had the abilities I'd discovered in myself while growing up. Of course, my great-grandmother had passed on years before, but it would have been comforting to know as a teenager with special abilities that there had been others like me in the family.

In my teenage years, I never really related to the average girl, as I was introverted and always felt so different. Of course I didn't understand the intuitive abilities I had at that time, and the visions I was having not only confused me but also scared me.

Since no one in my life understood why I was experiencing these visions, I thought there was something wrong with me.

* * *

At around the age of nineteen, my dates used to come and pick me up at my parents' house and then take me to dinner or the movies. I was young, vibrant and filled with unrealistic romantic ideas and beliefs. I was, in other words, very naïve and living in a complete fantasy world. I had no idea that most of my dates were going to spin any lie they could, just to get into my pants. I was completely blind to the fact that most young men did not want to have a serious relationship with a female, they just wanted sex. I would often get hurt and confused about why a certain young man would not call me after the first couple of dates. I didn't realize that if I didn't do the 'deed' with them, they would simply vanish into thin air, never to be seen again.

When we are younger, it isn't easy to listen to our intuition, because we have less life experience. In my case, I did not wish to listen to it, as I basically didn't care. My self-esteem was very low, and as I had little respect for myself, it was easy for many men to treat me unkindly. My confidence was at rock bottom and I was not able to defend myself or stand up for my divine rights. Basically, men walked all over me.

* * *

Four of my friends and I used to enjoy going to nightclubs. We were all studying and we wanted to let our hair down. With much excitement, we'd head to the city and party into the early hours of the morning. I would always sense the energy very strongly in these clubs, and as I was still young, I was unable to understand why I would become drained and sometimes unwell the next day. I was extremely against the idea of taking drugs and I was also unaware of the many young people who were taking them in these bars. I had never even experienced the sensation of marijuana, speed or ecstasy, and I never wanted to. As I danced with my friends, the energy around me was buzzing, and as I was more sensitive to energy than others, I would sometimes feel as if I was on a high. I thought it was just the atmosphere, and my endorphins were giving me that rush. I had no idea that it was the drugs and alcohol in the air—and in many of those around me—that I was sensing so strongly. People who have strong psychic abilities are always more sensitive to their environments than are others.

* * *

The strange thing was that I actually did meet my first true love at one of these sleazy bars. He was definitely one of the exceptions. Michael was standing with some male friends at the bar ordering some drinks. He was tall and handsome. He kept looking over at me and I confidently approached him. This was certainly out of character for me. Not my usual way of meeting a man, but Michael was so handsome. He seemed to stand out from the rest of the crowd, and I couldn't help myself. I leaned over the bar, and as he was talking to one of his friends, I introduced myself. Of course, I tried my best to be as casual as possible. Instead, my heart was beating rapidly, and I laughed a little too awkwardly. We ended up talking for hours in the bar. He asked me for my phone number and this time, he actually kept calling me and asking me out on dates, even after he was well aware that he was not going to get some serious action straight away.

Michael would stay in my life for a long time, and I thought of him as my angel during those years. Sometimes, people come into our lives to help us become stronger and that was exactly what he did. When people ask me today about my first true love, I can honestly say that he was not a bad man. I know that I broke his heart by leaving him for a new way of life, but we had both grown so much that we needed to go our separate ways. We were there for one another during those five years and I don't regret one minute of the time we spent together. It had been our destiny to meet, and I thank my angels for bringing him into my life at the time I needed him most.

However, Michael was finding it difficult to accept my new work. He had been happy with me selling fashion and was surprised that I would even consider becoming a psychic. He had seen me read natural health books and spiritual material, but he thought it was just a hobby. Michael tried desperately to accept my new line of work, as he didn't wish to let me go, but I could see it wasn't easy for him.

Even though I was the one who had left him, even though I was one hundred per cent certain that he was no longer for me, my heart was still breaking. I had known this beautiful soul for so many years and to suddenly have to leave him, because my intuition was telling me to, was so painful.

Before I broke it off, I had been through a period of complete denial. I recall him coming around to visit me at home. My mother answered the door. I couldn't make myself come down the stairs of our two-story home. It felt like I was being forced against my will. I finally made my way down to greet him, and even had to force a smile. We went to the movies that night. That would be our very last night out together. I still didn't have the ability to tell him the truth and I was scared that just maybe I would be making the biggest mistake of my life if I said a final goodbye.

The angel cards that kept falling out of my deck whenever I desperately needed some guidance, all pointed towards me moving forward and breaking free. I still didn't fully trust the cards, as I hadn't had much experience using them at that point in my life. Yet every single time I sat down to see what angel cards came through for me, they were always the same cards about breaking free from someone. My intuition was strongly guiding me away from this man, but as I had adored him for such a long part of my life, I couldn't get my head around the idea of leaving him for good.

Since I didn't wish to listen to my intuition, my body began trying to give me the message. I began experiencing incredibly sharp abdominal pains. I was even rushed to hospital while sleeping over at Michael's place. The pains in my stomach were horrific that night and the doctor who examined me explained to me that I had a severe case of chronic irritable bowel syndrome. This whole scenario with Michael was placing enormous pressure on me, and as I hadn't had the courage to leave him, my body was now paying the price. Sometimes when you don't want to listen to your intuition, something will happen in an extreme way to make you finally open your eyes and take the hint. My stomach cramps were telling me that if I didn't break away from this man, my health could get much worse.

So, I finally had the courage and strength to say goodbye to him for the very last time. It was one of the worst days of my life, but I had to be strong for both of us and make that final decision to go our separate ways. I could no longer see a future for our relationship. When you become familiar with someone, their voice, their touch and their own special, unique ways, it isn't easy to let them go, especially when they have loved you with all their heart.

I remember crying my eyes out alone in my bedroom. The pain was unbearable. I could still, however, hear my angels whispering to me that it was going to be okay. Even through the tears and the sadness, the angels were comforting me. Suddenly, my mind flashed back to about three years previously. Michael and I had been together for two years at that point. I recall arguing in the middle of the street, late at night. We had attended one of his work functions and I had been furious about something which had occurred at this party. He wanted to make it up to me, so he dragged me into a florist that was still open at that time of night. It was a little shop and as soon as we both entered, I got a funny feeling inside. This florist had music playing in the background and I recognized the song as one that Michael and I had agreed on playing for our first dance when we eventually got married.

Michael was very drunk, which was part of the reason for our fight, and when the lady handed me the flowers he had paid for, she looked me directly in the eyes. Since Michael was so drunk and had already stepped out of the shop, he didn't hear what she said to me. I did, however, and was thoroughly confused. "He is not for you. He will make you a stronger person, but you will meet someone else," she said.

Now, if he had been calling me awful names and screaming at me in front of her, I may have understood her words as simply words of concern. Yet she had never met us before and she was telling me he was not right for me. I blushed awkwardly and said goodbye, and somehow brushed her words aside. I must have forgotten about them over the next three years. When you love someone, a prediction from a stranger selling flowers will no doubt fall on deaf ears.

Only now, as I was crying on this bedroom floor, did her words resonate strongly with me. Now that I had actually left Michael, what that lady had told me three years ago in the tiny flower shop helped me to realize that I had made the best decision to move on. Her insight and her strong intuition that night confirmed to me that there was someone else out there for me. In the darkness of my heart breaking in two, I was so thankful for the florist's wisdom and her ability to foretell what my eyes had not been ready to see back then.

I heard through the grapevine that Michael met and fell in love with another girl two years after we broke up. I heard that he married her and they had a child together. I know they are living in the house that I was going to move into with him. I am happy for him. I am happy for her. More importantly, I am so happy that I was strong enough to break away.

Affirmation: "*I believe in myself and I believe in miracles.*"

Copy the affirmation on the prior page as many times as you wish.

CHAPTER 4

Earth angels

Some men don't wish to date a psychic. As soon as you mention that you can see through people and look into the future, they simply freak out. When people discover that you are psychic, they automatically believe you can read their mind as soon as you meet them and that you basically know everything about them. They feel you should know things like their names, or how old they are, or even what they just had for lunch. Intuitives can't read every single detail about a person, as we are only human; but more importantly, we are mainly here to help people on their paths. Our main purpose is to predict what a person's future holds; however, it is also to predict health concerns and career issues, so that people can move forward more quickly and easily, with our guidance. So, I apologize if I don't know what your name is or the last thing you had to eat, but really, I just don't care. I have more important things to predict.

At the first meeting, many of my clients tell me they were expecting me to look different. I understand exactly what they mean, as some people carry the belief that intuitives all dress in black and have grey hair. They believe that we all work behind a curtain, and when we pull it back, we come out dressed in long, spooky dresses, with wild hair that hasn't been brushed for days. Apparently, our eyes should look like they are popping out of our heads, and as we slowly usher them into the room to tell their fortune, they should almost trip over our black cat, which seemed to come out of nowhere. You must know what I am talking about, as all psychics are supposed to own a black cat, right? Well, guess what? I have a white cat. That's right, and I also get my hair done at a proper salon, with—wait for it—blonde highlights! Yes, I like to try to look sexy, and I even get facials.

Now I might come across as a kind of bimbo psychic, and at one point, due to being small-busted, I did consider a boob job— but the fact is, I do have brains. Many of my clients even consider me to be very wise. My mother might disagree with them, but that's because many of us can seem very vague. We can leave our keys in the car, and the number of times I have had to call the RACV to help me retrieve them is unbelievable—as they have told me themselves. Thank God I now need only press the button on the little gadget to automatically lock the doors, so I always remember to have my keys with me. These new types of locks are a psychic's dream, as we can forget things so easily. Some people also assume that we don't get manicures or do lady-like things. I wonder if that's why many men are shocked when I tell them that I am a psychic. 'Are you for real? You don't look like one!'

Many people find it hard to understand that angels are really out there, and that we, as intuitives, can tap into the higher dimensions and experience what it's like to connect with them. Some people just don't wish to accept what they can't see with the human eye, so I understand their hesitancy to trust me and other psychics who also have this ability. What if you could believe that you were protected at all times? What if you knew that God and the angels were there, every single step of the way, guiding you lovingly and telling you that you were safe? Wouldn't you wish to have that? Well, I believe I am blessed every single moment of my life, as that is exactly how I feel. I thank God every day for my gift and my abilities. I sometimes have beautiful, strong visions of the other side. I consider myself very fortunate to have this ability and definitely do not take my gift for granted.

* * *

Some people believe Intuitives should not be allowed to make predictions of any sort for others and that people should be able to make up their own minds. I can't agree, as I have found that even though everyone makes up their own mind in the end on certain issues, some people are just completely lost and have given up hope. Intuitives help to bring more light and hope into their lives again, so they can believe that things are generally going to be okay for them.

My readings usually confirm to clients that they are doing the right thing. It basically validates that they are making the correct decisions in life. If a session confirms to a client that they are on the right path when everything feels so overwhelming, then they can have faith in the angels and guides that are watching over them. If they are not on the right track and possibly on the way to a self-destructive path, it is my job to help steer them in a happier direction.

A session can also assist clients to discover their own intuitive abilities and help them to connect with their own angels. This way, they don't need to continue to see a psychic to get their answers. This has been the case for some of my own clients. This does not mean that they all end up becoming a professional psychic or healer; in most cases, it is simply for their own personal benefit.

On some rare occasions, due to the information from the angels not being very clear, or even because the client is not ready to hear the information, an intuitive can give inaccurate information to the client. As much as you want to help the client, there are those awkward, frustrating sessions in which the guidance and information is not coming through. So, you must tell the client that it is not their fault but the information is not being revealed clearly in the session.

I can get so frustrated after these sessions. Even though they are rare, I believe that I have both embarrassed myself and also let my client down. I feel that I haven't fulfilled their needs. I never charge the client in these cases, as they deserve honesty and accuracy in a reading. I also would not even wish to be in the industry unless the majority of my readings were considered very accurate and beneficial to my clients. Since no one's future is written in stone, many of my readings have come true, while others have changed due to free will.

Every psychic is different and chooses to read for their clients in a way that is comfortable to them. Some of us are drawn to tarot cards, some prefer reading with angel cards, and others feel that they can read their clients best with coffee cups or a crystal ball. Each of us have our own personal style and we work in a way that is best for ourselves and our clients.

I read angel oracle cards to give guidance to my clients and I read people's jewelry to pick up on their energy. I love healing the person sitting in front of me and seeing their life change after a session. I often have women coming more than once, returning even three or four times, as my abilities lie in helping people to have more confidence and courage in times of major distress.

When a client comes to see me, I lead them into my office. The client takes a seat and I ask them for their first name and their date of birth. I also ask them for their watch or another piece of jewelry, which I then hold in my left hand, so that I can sense their energy. I begin to shuffle a deck of angel cards while the client closes their eyes and thinks of questions to which they wish the session to provide answers.

I then proceed to place about ten of the angel cards on the

table before the client. What occurs next is called 'channeling', as I sense things come through that I believe need to be conveyed to the client. None of this is scary in any way for me or my client. In fact, the entire session is very relaxing and everything is conveyed in the most gentle and caring manner. Picture, if you will, a counselor with her client—just add the angel cards, jewelry and 'visions' to the session. The guidance is never forced upon the client. It is given to them, and they can decide to take it or leave it, by their own free will. Most clients, however, resonate strongly with the information and find that it helps them to keep moving forward in life. Psychics are also known as Intuitives, Sensitives and Empaths. I prefer using these terms, as they describe our capabilities and clients relate better to them.

Affirmation: "I am worthy of great love. I love myself."

Copy the affirmation on the prior page as many times as you wish.

CHAPTER 5

Dating an Intuitive

I met him at a bar. He was standing there looking very handsome and sexy, so I stared back at his intense gaze. Finally, he approached me. He introduced himself as Daniel. I started to feel a little awkward, as he looked me up and down as if to say, 'I like what I see'. I asked him a few questions that I had probably asked many men in this situation. He answered and proceeded to ask me some questions, which I eagerly answered. We began to laugh together and I felt very relaxed with this man. He then asked me *the* question: "So, what do you do for work?" I took a deep breath.

"I am a natural healer," I answered nervously.

"Oh yeah, so what does that involve exactly?" he asked with eyes large and round.

"I'm an intuitive counselor. I help and guide women."

"Intuitive? What does that mean?" He frowned.

"Well, I guide them. I used to run meditation classes but I'm currently having a break from doing them." Somehow, the word 'psychic' was too taboo for me to use at this moment. I thought it might—well, scare him off completely.

"Sounds very interesting," he replied, as he stared at me again with those eyes. "So, do you want to go out on a date with me?"

We did go out on that date. He was waiting outside a café I had never been to before. I smiled at him as we both entered the trendy little café, and the waiter handed us some menus and walked us over to a table. "So, how are you? How was your day?" my date asked as we both sat down.

"You know, just an average sort of day," I lied miserably. *I really want to say I had a very interesting day. I predicted things for a client and helped guide her with her relationship. Somehow, it just doesn't feel like the best answer.*

We chatted for a long time and I found myself drawn to him. Then I told him the truth, "Daniel, I have to be honest with you. I am a psychic."

The truth shocked him. He kind of pulled back a little and stared at me in a strange way. I didn't like the look in his eyes. *Maybe he's looking at me strangely because he thinks I'm strange.*

"Oh, I didn't know you were a psychic. I don't care what you do for work, as long as you're not a stripper."

Why do they always say this? "Daniel, so you are okay with me giving guidance and making future predictions? I use angel cards for my clients and I recently thought about getting a crystal ball." *He's looking at me now with an even stranger expression on his face. His eyes seem like they're ready to pop out of his head.*

"Oh, I see." He gulped. "That's fine. Like I said, whatever you do, it doesn't bother me. It doesn't bother me at all." I found out very soon that it *did* bother him, as he never called me again. Apparently strippers and psychics were not on his list of future partners.

* * *

There was another incident in which my dinner date couldn't sit still once he discovered the truth about my work. He looked at me with fear in his eyes and said, "So, does that mean you can read every single thought I'm thinking? It makes me really nervous that you can pick up on my thoughts."

What does this man have to hide? Why would he be so insecure if I really was doing that? The fine hairs lifted on the back of my neck and my stomach quivered. Sitting across from him, I was definitely not reading his thoughts—it's just not that simple. My heart sank. This date was a complete waste of time. He wouldn't be calling me for a second date, nor did I want him to, as I felt he would be untrustworthy. What secrets did he have? Or was he scared that I could see he just wanted to use me and get into my pants?

I reiterate that certain individuals have the wrong idea about empaths. Many believe that as soon as we meet them, we can telepathically read their minds and sense everything about them. Believe me when I say that I certainly don't wish to do this, as I have much better things to do with my life. This is why private sessions are arranged with an Empath, so that it is much easier for accurate information to come through for the client.

* * *

I was single and I was dating. I didn't particularly hate it but I definitely did not love it, either. I had no choice but to get into the swing of dating, unless I wished to end up alone. When a psychic predicts that you will meet a certain fellow, they do not mean that he will appear at your front door, just like magic, with a bunch of flowers, and say, 'How about it?' They presume that you will muster the courage to have some girls' nights out on the town, or try internet dating, join other social networks, and even travel interstate or to foreign destinations. They know that if you put in the effort and time to try to meet your Mr. Right, then he will appear. If you just sit at home, lounging on the couch watching your favorite television shows, you may most likely miss out on meeting your destined match.

So, once again, I was getting ready for another night out with a man who had asked me to see a movie with him. This time, however, my intuition was telling me that this man was not the one for me. So, I stopped then and there, ceased applying my make-up and picked up my mobile phone to send him a message saying that I was unfortunately unable to make our date, as I had a bad migraine. The entire date would simply have been upsetting for me, having to sit there while knowing clearly that he was not the man for me.

On another occasion, I recall having that same feeling that a certain man was not for me; however, since I thought he was absolutely gorgeous, I completely ignored my intuition that time. I chose instead to gaze into my date's beautiful eyes. As we dated, the attraction between us grew. It turned out that this man had lost his dear mother to cancer. I recall that the moment I stepped foot in his stylish house, I immediately sensed her presence. I could see a photo of her on the mantelpiece not far from the entrance. She had been a very attractive lady. Her energy was very comforting and loving and there was a deep sense of peace in the house. She was definitely looking after her son. My intuition warned me not to fall head over heels for him, simply because on a higher level we were not compatible enough as lovers. Once again, I didn't wish to listen and I brushed it aside.

We got closer and during that time, I was able to bring mother and son together again. He was surprised by my ability to know so much about his mother in spirit. Soon after, however, the relationship started to break apart and we began to have problems. Of course, I should have listened to my intuition but I also believe that in this particular case, I was meant to ignore it. By having a brief romance with him, I brought more closure and happiness into his life. He was finally able to reconnect with his mother.

Affirmation: "I fall in love with life. I have lots of fun."

Copy the affirmation on the prior page as many times as you wish.

CHAPTER 6

Love and destiny

The new millennium has made it easy for us to date online, thanks to the wonderful technology of the internet. I took a huge leap of faith when I jumped on the 'net.

I liked the fact that you could choose a potential partner from a large range of photos and descriptions. Being an Intuitive made it even easier, as I simply followed my intuition, to take me to the photo and profile that would most likely suit me. It definitely helped to rule out any men who were not for me. It saved me from wasting my time and energy on a man who was completely incompatible with me. But it didn't mean that I was definitely going to marry the first man I dated, either. What it meant was that I would have something in common with him at least, and he wouldn't be a complete loser or nutcase.

I had other single friends around my age who were anxious to meet their own Mr. Right. I told them not to worry. I am a big believer in positive thinking and destiny, so I understood how negativity would not help the issue and might also prolong the interval before meeting their true love. Sometimes I could get really frustrated, but I never let that feeling last long, as my guides always stepped in to say that it wasn't my time yet. I told my guides that I trusted them, although I would love to meet the right man as soon as possible.

* * *

My heart had been broken many times and I had broken many hearts, too. I hadn't met 'him' yet but when I did, I knew that I would understand why my angels believed that I had to wait. I would fully comprehend why I needed to be more patient than most women my age.

I was sitting on a warm sandy beach; the sea was healing, with its crystal blue waters sending me love and light. My heart skipped a beat as I turned my head to see a tall, handsome stranger walking his dog. I felt a little awkward as he turned to gaze in my direction and I noticed him blush ever so slightly.

He smiled at me and made a comment about how I was lucky to have the entire shore to myself. I was pleased to see that he had noticed me and I said something—well, anything to keep his attention on me. He was a writer. He had that dream to write a book and his determination made me weak at the knees. I was happy to get to know this attractive, intelligent man as he plonked himself down beside me. We talked for hours before I finally stood up and, brushing the sand off my back, I told him it was time for me to head home. He invited me out to dinner that very same night. I excitedly accepted his invitation and my heart beat fast as I returned home to prepare for my date.

He turned up at my door and we enjoyed a beautiful, romantic dinner at a restaurant right near the ocean. Like a scene straight out of a romance novel, it seemed too good to be true—because it was. I only saw him for a couple more dates. Then, suddenly, we both knew that we were not right for one another. It only took three dates to realize this. We were both mature adults and in this world of dating, you didn't need very long before you had an inkling whether or not the relationship could continue. I know this wasn't case for everyone, but maybe as I was so intuitive, it certainly felt this way to me. It still made me sad and heartbroken that I'd even met him, that he'd crossed my path. Where was that cupid's arrow heading? To whom? Didn't the angels understand my frustration about not having a partner? Had they not seen how much pain I had already been through in waiting patiently for Mr. Right?

* * *

I'd have to give it another go with another man soon enough, and yes, it might once again result in a broken heart. This is where people would jump in and point their fingers at me and say, "You are a psychic, how come you don't know when you will meet your man? Shouldn't you know that?" I would answer with no hesitation that psychics sometimes just couldn't know things. I was aware that I absolutely would meet the man of my dreams but not how or when, and I had faith that my angels would send him to me. My angels would not leave me stranded. They had a plan and it didn't matter that I didn't understand how it would turn out, all that mattered was that I had faith that it would. If I was able to see everything about how my life would turn out, where would there be the fun and excitement? Life is full of surprises and I wanted some of that, too. However, I might still throw a little tantrum and get frustrated—I had needs and wants like any human being, and sometimes that lack of faith would definitely creep in.

Everyone creates a large part of their own destiny, I believe that Intuitives can only see so much of a person's future, only some pieces of the puzzle. We all have free will and nothing is set in stone. Thoughts and belief systems also create our destiny. These days, many Intuitives work on healing their clients, so that they can be more positive and healthier. They teach and empower their clients to create the best future for themselves.

Intuitives like myself only predict things that we are guided to see for our clients and in some cases, we will only be shown what the client can handle and what they need to experience next. We wonder what the angels have in store for us. So, sometimes a reader will simply guide us gently into that next phase of our lives, bringing more assurance that everything will be fine in the next few chapters of our lives.

This doesn't mean that I haven't been able to predict my client's true love, the one they walk down the aisle with and marry. Many of my clients have informed me that they were surprised that I was able to foresee their husband well before he arrived in their lives, describing him to a tee. Romance and love relationships appear to be my specialty, as I have clients that have a reading with me simply because they heard through a friend or a relation, that I can assist them in the area of love. I frequently have the ability to see if a couple is experiencing difficulties and they need to work on healing the relationship, or they have both had enough and have separated and gone their own way. I give them guidance during this difficult time. I am also known for advising clients on how to help manifest a special person into their lives.

Affirmation: "I manifest a beautiful, caring and loyal partner."

Copy the affirmation on the prior page as many times as you wish.

CHAPTER 7

When an angel answers

Maybe part of my reason for still being a single gal was because I had heard anything and everything you could imagine when it came to matters of the heart. Imagine hearing, day after day, incredible secrets that your closest friends or family would never dream of telling you. The fact that so many of my clients had been cheated on and lied to was unbelievable, and I really felt for them. Many of them were so crushed by the experience that they found it difficult to trust anyone ever again.

I believe that what goes around comes around, so I don't understand why so many people are cheating on their partner in this day and age. Doesn't anyone believe in the karmic principles? Or are they so driven by lust that they simply don't care? Do they not worry about whether they are hurting others? Drugs, lies, cheating and sex—it all sounds like some kind of best-selling novel or your average TV show, but these were the true lives of many of my clients. Not the ones who actually came to see me face-to-face but those who consulted me through the phone readings I had with women and men who knew that I could not see them or identify them in public. Most were interstate or overseas, far away from ever being caught out. These phone calls were connected to a company I used to work for based in Sydney. The call would first come through to their phone lines and then it would connect to my home phone in Melbourne. So, I had no idea who these callers were. They were strangers, completely hidden to my eyes, which was why they were able to air all their dirty laundry to me.

Sometimes I was intrigued by their stories and I felt like I was being allowed into the most private areas of my clients' lives. One woman called me on a regular basis to get guidance. She was involved with a married man and she was married herself. She didn't understand how this had happened to her, since she had always been so conservative and cheating was not something that she had ever condoned. This particular man seemed to have some kind of hold on her. He was very unhappily married and he told her that he was no longer in love with his wife. He convinced her that he no longer wished to be with his wife but the only thing that had kept him from leaving her were his two beloved children. He didn't wish to disappoint them and he believed he was doing the right thing by staying in the marriage. Yet he needed her to fully trust in him and believe him when he told her that he would be with her in an instant if he could.

Sounds like a scene from *Days of Our Lives*—more like a phone conversation with one of my clients that I nicknamed 'Days of Our Lies'. This was a typical story that I could hear up to four times a day doing phone readings for your average suburban wife. If you don't believe that your next-door neighbor could be screwing another woman's husband, then you are definitely living in fantasy land!

Now, I don't mean to shock and alarm you so that you go and tie up your husbands to stop them from running amuck, but this cheating stuff is not just happening on television soapies or in 'Hollywood'. These people had really major issues that they needed to heal and deal with, and the majority of them were not happily married or did not understand the concept of 'having morals'. Unfortunately, I was dealing with these women and men whose lives were filled with so much sadness that they believed that this kind of relationship was their only chance for some 'real happiness'. Or some of them just didn't care about others' feelings and had no morals. Since their lives were messed up, it seemed perfectly fine for them to mess up someone else's life.

I tried never to judge them for their actions, as we were taught to keep an open mind about anyone's problems and the way they chose to live their lives. Don't think that I wasn't frustrated that people were losing their morals—or maybe even their minds— though. It didn't stop me from speaking my mind at times and tell them what I really thought.

One possible reason I had been more careful in regards to marriage and relationships in general was because my ears had heard more about debauchery than many people would hear in a lifetime. I knew, though, that I still had to remain positive about the idea of a trustworthy partner, and that not all relationships were doomed for unhappiness and divorce. So, I was not going to believe that all men were cheaters. I truly did believe that there were men who respected women and did not wish to hurt them.

There were also some amazing and kind-hearted people who called me through these particular phone lines; clients who were sensitive by nature and in need of some guidance; clients who were successful and business-minded, who desired some direction in their career. One man who used to call was a successful restaurant owner. He travelled frequently overseas to exotic places. His social agenda was hectic and involved mingling with high profile businessmen and women from all around the globe. Not one of these business acquaintances would ever guess that he carried a deck of 'oracle angel cards' in his suitcase.

Another client was involved in politics and journalism. Occasionally, she rang me for direction if things were overwhelming and stressful on the work front. Another lady called because she had issues with a man she was in love with. He lived interstate and she missed him terribly but due to her responsibilities and circumstances as a single mother, she was unable to be with him.

One woman was physically and mentally abused by her husband, but she didn't have the emotional strength to leave him. She had three children to him and was very concerned about her financial situation if she left. I always suggested people in these circumstances should attend counseling.

A male caller had been physically unwell for a number of years and was healing. His health improved incredibly due to the help of a talented specialist he was seeing. He was excited to re-enter the workforce soon and live a much better way of life.

These are only a handful of the callers I used to deal with. Their personal stories remind me of how similar everyone really is. Their pain and problems are really no different from everyone else's.

Affirmation: "I embrace my sensitivity. I am sacred."

Copy the affirmation on the prior page as many times as you wish.

CHAPTER 8

Light after darkness

I was having a drink in a cozy little café when I saw him. He looked the same. He hadn't changed much. He was still strikingly handsome. As soon as he handed me his business card, I had a flashback.

He had broken my heart. He had wanted to go back to his ex-girlfriend. He told me that he loved her, that he had always loved her. He explained to me that he still cared for me though. Then he had left.

I never saw him again, that is up until now, in this trendy café. My girlfriend had been running late, and I had been waiting patiently for her to arrive. I looked at the ring on his finger, as we both entered into conversation. He was now married. Married to the girl he had left me for. They had two little children.

The business card lay on the table untouched. He wasn't giving it to me for any other reason, but to apparently keep in touch. He said if I ever needed someone to speak to, I could just give him a call. If I hadn't been sitting waiting for my friend, I would have been able to just get up and walk out the door. Unfortunately, I had to sit there until he decided to leave.

I didn't offer him a seat. I was single at the time, so I could have easily have taken up his offer. Instead, I thought of his wife and his children. They had hearts that could easily be broken. He had been my past. He was definitely not going to be my future in any way. He looked at me, hoping to get some kind of response. I looked at him with pity. The business card fell on the floor. One of the waitresses accidently knocked it. He didn't pick it up. I certainly wasn't going to.

He blushed, then quickly said goodbye. He finally exited the café. When my friend arrived, she apologized for running late, there had been lots of traffic. I hugged her and as she had seen my ex-boyfriend talking to me, she asked who that man was. I replied that he was no one important. Then we both ordered our meals.

* * *

I was in a fragile state of mind. Let's say that I was still hurting tremendously. Some of my experiences while moving from house to house were extremely eye-opening and very distressing. I found certain individuals to be unfair and dishonest when it came to matters of paying rent and sharing expenses. I discovered with shock that they had no idea of the meaning of the word 'respect'. As far as they were concerned, I was just another person who was renting out their apartment. If a heater suddenly broke down, the fact that I was suffering with the flu in the middle of winter was not something that seemed to bother them in the slightest. I was still attracting souls that were taking advantage of me and it made me furious. Instead of keeping calm and not saying anything to them, I spoke up. I was not a very happy lady from being walked all over and I was confused that people could actually be so cruel.

Some of these individuals lied about their financial issues and would try to get more money from me than they deserved. I was losing faith in people more and more and I didn't wish to suppress my emotions any longer. I stood my ground. I wasn't coping with life in general and I felt that people were overstepping their boundaries with me.

In a matter of only two years, I moved house up to six times. I wasn't feeling very secure and stable within, so this, unfortunately, manifested in my housing situation. One of the angels I was calling on each time I moved was Archangel Gabrielle[1]. When I would start having strong visions of this angel, I knew she was around, warning me that once again, I would have to move.

I needed this angel comforting me more than ever. Unless you have been in a similar situation, in which you have moved many times, you cannot understand the pain and exhaustion your mind and body can experience. To put it quite simply, I believed I was having a mild nervous breakdown. Due to my health issues, my financial situation was also not so great, so I felt shuffled around from house to house. My choice of housemates was not very clever and we tended to clash in our beliefs about money and other living arrangements.

My parents assisted me with my finances by paying off my large credit card debt and I was so grateful for this. They had also been very generous in other ways in the past. They were there for me whenever I needed assistance.

Things seemed completely hopeless. It was a struggle for me not to fall into the victim game and I felt I was living a painful existence. I was 29 years of age and once again, I was going through a difficult path. I was 29, so I refused to move back home. I needed to do this on my own.

I had offers from men during this time to go and live with them. I was aware this was a better option for me in regards to my living arrangements; however, I knew deep down that it would be worse for me in the long run to move in. I didn't love them

---

[1] There is much debate surrounding the Archangel Gabrielle's/Gabriel's gender. Gabrielle is described using male pronouns in both the Old and New Testament of the Bible, Koran, and the Dead Sea Scrolls. But paintings of the Annunciation assign Gabrielle a feminine face and body and flowing feminine gown. Gabrielle is attributed with both feminine properties (nurturing, kind, compassionate, and gentle) and also male properties (strong, supportive, and motivational).

enough to make such a drastic move. Some of these men were very caring and genuine but my heart wasn't there and I was an emotional wreck, so I didn't have the stamina to commit to a man in such a way. I didn't wish to use someone just to have an easier, more comfortable way of life. Some of these men would definitely have been able to provide me with a fantastic lifestyle, with their beautiful, large homes and fancy cars; however, I wasn't going to go and live with them unless I really loved them.

The amount of times that I had packed my belongings and moved into a new home was heart-breaking, but each time, I saw Archangel Gabrielle standing there above me and I would relax. She was there telling me that it would be okay and that this was all leading me to a better path. She was there protecting me and I couldn't have made it through without her. I knew that eventually, I would be safer and happier. She was leading me to a more positive outcome in the end. This is what angels do for us. This one angel held my hand during the times that I wanted out of this life. She kept me going when I felt like I couldn't see the light anymore.

The best part about asking for help from above was that it brought back a sense of empowerment and faith. When you know that you are being watched over and protected, you sense that things are going to be okay. You are more positive about your future and you have plenty of faith that your prayers will be answered.

The dating game is not always easy for the single gal or guy, with its painful break-ups and heartaches. Many women and men can become disheartened and wish to give up on finding their ideal partner. They become quite negative and make constant comments about how they will never find the right partner. When you have strong faith that you are being guided and watched over, you believe that you will definitely meet your soulmate, and you know your love life is more than okay.

* * *

I was at another popular bar in the city with a close female friend of mine. Late into the night, a guy plopped himself down next to me on the couch where I was comfortably seated. My girlfriend was completely lost in the eyes of a hunky man standing beside the bar, both of them downing drinks. I had no choice but to talk to this guy sitting next to me. We started with the small talk and he began to bore me the very instant he opened his mouth. I lied to him and told him that I had just started to date someone. I thought he would instantly get the hint and leave me be, but he promptly commented that he was also casually dating another woman, so he just wanted to chat as friends. Was there any harm in that? What could I say to that? He started to talk about his career and the state of his wallet—and I don't mean if it was made of leather and imported. He also went on to brag about his ability to get girls very easily.

I then told him about my work and how I read angel cards as a living. How I could see things that others couldn't see. The expression on his face said it all. He slightly rolled his eyes and said, "Oh, that's bullshit. I don't believe in gypsies. Many of them are back in my home country of Ukraine, where I was born."

I defended myself instantly and said, "We are not full of bullshit. What I do, I am very proud of, and I have helped many people with my gift."

He seemed a little embarrassed, his face flushing a vivid red, and he apologized, and he then was interested in finding out more about my work. I continued to talk to him, with the understanding that some people were still living in the dark ages where psychics were considered the outcasts of society. Suddenly, I had a strong vision of two gold wedding rings before him, so I went with my feeling and asked, "When are you getting married?"

That's when his eyes widened and he said in a shocked voice, "How did you know that? I am engaged and will be getting married at the end of this year."

I explained to him the vision I'd had.

He'd lied when he'd originally told me that he was 'casually' dating another woman. Being engaged was definitely not something I would consider 'casual dating'! I think most guys would agree with me on this one, as the majority of them freak out at the simple mention of the word 'engagement'. This particular man seemed to treat me with much more respect after my vision and I believe I may have changed his views on my fellow 'gypsies'.

* * *

One of my friends thought that a man she knew would be the perfect guy for me. She had a strong feeling that we would be compatible and complement each other in many ways. She unfortunately couldn't have been more wrong. My kind, considerate—did I mention married—friend was concerned for me. She, of course, wasn't the only one who was worried that I was miserable and lonely, just because I didn't have a man beside me, holding my hand, taking me out for nice dinners. It seemed everyone was getting nervous for my future and believed that I was headed for a very lonely one.

So, what else could I do, but accept her invitation to a party she held one warm Saturday evening at her home. Lucas was there. He was wearing a black ribbed, fitted jumper teamed with trendy, black jeans. My friend had good taste at least. Lucas had a beautiful smile and deep, green eyes that pierced right through me. I couldn't help but want to talk to him, so was very grateful when my friend finally introduced us. We surprisingly got along well and I was excited when this handsome man offered to take me out for a date.

We started seeing each other on a regular basis and I enjoyed Lucas's company. Time passed very quickly. Over intimate dinners we became closer.

Lucas lived in an apartment in the city. I had to drive to his place and then from there, we were going to go to the casino to watch a movie together. There was something that I really liked about him. I felt drawn to him. The only problem being that he found it difficult to accept my work and my beliefs. Besides his inability to connect with my work, he was a really nice man and tried to understand it. He was your traditional Italian man with a very loving upbringing and strong Catholic beliefs.

Sometimes the signs from my angels are so strong that I can't ignore them, even if I try. For some reason on this particular freezing cold night, I could not for the life of me find the front door to his apartment. There were about fifteen other apartments on his block and my memory had suddenly gone blank and I couldn't recall the number of his place. The angels were definitely giving me strong warning signs that he was not for me.

I was too embarrassed to call him and ask him what his number was, as I had been to his place ten times and he would have thought that I was plain stupid. I was taking too long to find it and I was beginning to feel incredibly stressed. He finally rang my mobile and I answered, telling him that I was extremely tired and hung over from the night before, and I couldn't recall the number of his apartment. He laughed. I was suddenly on his list of all the dumb women he had dated—in fact, I am certain I was on the very top.

Once again, my angels had been correct. That very night, he was talking about how much he adored me but he didn't know if he could ever accept my work. He was finding it too much of a challenge. He told me that he couldn't accept the fact that I was a psychic. He had tried his best and he was afraid of hurting me in the long run. He didn't mean to disrespect me by not having the same beliefs. I couldn't even look at him. I knew that it was over then and there. My abilities were not something that were difficult to love. They were not just a part of me, they 'were' me! I couldn't comprehend where I had gone wrong. He was everything I had searched for in a man, minus the biggest factor— the acceptance of my work. I remember crying, silently wishing that I had not been given this gift, begging for it to be taken from me. I wanted it to go away and never come back, only because I wanted this man so much. I couldn't see how foolish my thinking was. I craved his love and affection. I longed for his acceptance. I wished to be 'normal'. I wanted my abilities to wash away into the sea, never to return. Sometimes in my life, my gifts made me feel so different to others, that I believed I was better off without them. Sometimes I wished I'd never been born with them.

The angels were showing me the way once again. This time, I headed straight for the door and it was very easy to find my way back to my car. Tears were streaming down my face and it was raining heavily outside. My crying was uncontrollable. I clutched my heart with my hand and could feel it breaking in two. I was a complete mess.

The thing was, I wasn't really crying over just losing this man. I was very tired and emotionally drained from having to allow men into my life, only to have them leave so quickly. I couldn't believe how many men I had dated, and how many had broken my heart. I couldn't comprehend how many hearts I had also broken. I was sad because I'd put my heart and soul into certain relationships, and it seemed like a complete waste of time and energy. Here I was once again, saying goodbye to another man. Lucas was just another male in whom I had invested my time. I'd had enough of investing my time in men. My heart felt so vulnerable. I couldn't take any more.

* * *

It happened completely by accident. I was not intending to meet someone that night and I certainly wasn't in the mood for another man. I recall that night feeling a little different from most. I remember the atmosphere being more exciting and more inviting than it had been in a long time. I wasn't at the bar looking for anyone special. I'd just gone to have a fun and relaxed time with my girlfriend, and amongst the crowd, I saw John, a very handsome and down-to-earth guy. He was European. As I had tried to avoid European men, due to what I had perceived as their lack of open-mindedness, my first words to him were not very inviting. "Look, I really don't believe I am for you. I am too kooky for you."

John's words were a pleasant shock to me. "That's okay, I like 'kooky'."

He definitely proved that to me over the coming weeks, as we became closer and closer. He had a very caring and understanding nature, and I found out how open-minded and spiritual this Greek man really was. I had known him in many lifetimes and it just felt like he 'got' me, whereas so many men didn't. I kept checking with my angels, asking them to please give me a very clear sign if John wasn't for me. But no sign ever came. It surprised me, as I was so used to sensing that the man was not for me and I was certain that at any given moment, my intuition would step in and tell me that I had to leave him—but lo and behold, it just didn't happen. My friends were all shocked and amazed that I was still with him three months later, and that I had my things packed, ready to move in with him. Things were definitely changing around me.

We had a strong, beautiful connection and I could finally just be myself. I knew that true peace lay in the art of loving and accepting myself. On this spiritual journey, I had been fortunate enough to discover that once I fully accepted myself, only then would a partner embrace every part of me.

I loved and adored John. The way he held me and hugged me brought me so much joy, and I was finally able to smile more. He was able to really connect with me and understand me. Our relationship was a very healing one and it helped me to grow in so many ways. I couldn't even bear to think of my life without him and the mere thought of him walking out on me was absolutely heart-breaking. I called him my 'angel'.

We laughed a lot and we made fun of each other in a light-hearted manner. I recall when we first met that it took him some time to get used to me and my psychic ways. One night while we were watching a movie together and cuddling up on the couch, the lights suddenly went off. John looked at me with panic all over his face. Through the dim light I could see his eyes were large, round and fixated. He said in a serious tone, "Did you do that?" Instead of feeling insulted by his comment, I couldn't stop laughing. As if I had nothing better to do than freak out the guy I was interested in by leaving us both in the dark. I wasn't aware that people thought psychics could do such a thing, and I was starting to believe that maybe I should learn how to. I think John was really trying his best to accept my work, yet he could still be completely freaked out by it.

Affirmation: "I have faith in my divine plan. I trust that all is happening for my highest good."

Copy the affirmation on the prior page as many times as you wish.

CHAPTER 9

Relationships and angel healing

Whenever John and I argue, it can be so distressing for me that I immediately call upon God and one of the angels, Archangel Raphael, who oversees relationship difficulties. I pray for him to immediately bring some clarity and peace to the situation. The Archangel Raphael always helps and there is a lot more harmony between John and myself after I have called him to our side. That doesn't mean our relationship is healed straight away. In some instances, depending on the argument, it has taken time to heal. Of course, you can only work alone on your relationship so much, and if only one of you is willing to put in the effort, sometimes it's best to move on. Both partners need to be willing to compromise and evolve where necessary.

John's ability to accept my gift and my intuitive beliefs has been amazing. He has proven to me how open-minded he is and just how much he loves me. It's the little things that I do as a natural healer and a psychic that intrigue John. For instance, when I sleep at night, I tend to have crystals under my pillow or beside me. They are healing for me and relax me if I have had a stressful day. I love my crystals and wear gemstones all the time. Not only do they look pretty, but the beautiful energy they emit can assist your health in many ways.

Affirmation: "I am positive in life. I am calm and content."

Copy the affirmation on the prior page as many times as you wish.

CHAPTER 10

Vows from the heart

If I wanted to marry John, I would be marrying into a Greek family. I loved John with all my heart, so I was willing to risk some of the consequences that came along with a 'psychic' entering into a family of traditional Greek heritage. It was definitely going to be a challenge for us.

The more I thought about it, the answer became very clear. I would continue to do my work whether others accepted me or not, and I would prove that Intuitives were just normal people with normal lives—and they would eventually be accepted for the gifted people they were.

* * *

The more we became united as a couple and spent more time in each other's arms, the more John was able to pick up on my thoughts and what I was feeling, without even saying one word. He often surprised me by saying exactly what I was thinking. He also didn't need to be a professional healer or connected to the natural healing industry to send healing energy into my body. He could just wrap his arms around me, and his love made me feel calmer and happier. He seemed to heal pain in my body and so I knew that he was definitely the man for me.

When John mentioned the word 'marriage' and told me that

71

he wanted to walk down the aisle with me, my heart did a little flip and it surprised me. I had never wanted to marry anyone. I'd had many other psychics tell me that I would meet the man of my dreams and I would definitely tie the knot. They also said I would remain with him for a long time. I used to shake my head in disbelief, as I wasn't interested in having a traditional wedding ceremony. I'd harbored no desire to get married and I'd felt a lot of fear about marrying, due to the large increase in divorces.

Having met and fallen in love with John, however, I started to visualize myself in a wedding dress. I realized I would like a simple church ceremony to make both sets of parents content. I was brought up as a Catholic and John was raised Greek Orthodox. Out of respect for John and our parents, I would definitely have a church ceremony. The reception after the church would be intimate and relaxed. I couldn't even begin to visualize a large traditional reception, with old-fashioned pillars at the front and 400 guests. Definitely not my kind of wedding. I wanted something elegant yet simple, and I wanted to invite people who John and I actually knew and were close to.

Affirmation: "I attract beautiful, loving people in my life. I am loving and caring."

Copy the affirmation on the prior page as many times as you wish.

CHAPTER 11

The power of positivity

We were on a plane travelling towards beautiful Fiji. John seemed very calm, considering he had an extreme fear of flying. He had flown many times as he loved visiting new places, but each time he had to board a plane, panic had set in. I'd sent him to a hypnotherapist and it seemed as if he had been able to work on releasing some of John's fear. Fiji was so serene and calm. I could see the beautiful, vast ocean surrounding the islands as our plane descended for landing. John's company had paid for the trip. They were definitely a generous company, though John and some others had worked extra hard for this reward. The group of people who had joined us on this holiday to paradise were absolutely lovely and had a great energy about them.

We went on amazing boat tours and the islands were so beautiful. The scenery was absolutely breathtaking. I was so grateful to be on this holiday. Just before our trip to paradise, I had felt a desperate urge to have a break from helping and guiding others. The sea salt was cleansing and I went for long walks along the beach.

I drank alcohol at night to help me 'socialize' more and get into the right atmosphere. My alcohol intake was not much in comparison to everyone else on the tour. I didn't wish to drink a lot, as once again, my body could only handle so much. After only one drink, the alcohol started to go to my head. Suddenly, I could sense myself becoming very dreamy and dizzy. My speech began to slur slightly and not make much sense. Of course, these were the normal effects of alcohol on one's body; the problem was that I had only drunk one glass of wine and already, the room was beginning to spin around me.

Yes, with only one drink, I can get very drunk. I am not exaggerating and John or any of my friends can tell you that one glass of wine can make me very dizzy, and burst into fits of laughter—I basically get the giggles and my vagueness can become very evident. That's all fine when you have your friends around you or it's just you and your partner who knows you very well and doesn't believe you have lost the plot. However, when you are having dinner with your boyfriend's bosses, you need to make a good impression. Unfortunately, that one drink at dinner with John's bosses made me very 'ditzy', and I was slurring my words way too much. I was definitely not acting very lady-like and I don't believe John's bosses were too impressed with my behavior.

Alcohol is best kept as far away as possible from people like me. Some people are just too sensitive and if they are not normally used to consuming large amounts of alcohol, it is better not to touch liquor on an important occasion such as dinner with the bosses. I knew that it was not a great idea, my intuition told me this, but sometimes you just want to have a drink—and it was only one glass. John didn't seem to handle his intake of alcohol, either—not many people can handle ten alcoholic drinks. John definitely proved that to his bosses and workmates on the very first night of the holiday.

He started to get a little moody at the end of the night, so I went back to our hotel room and as I was very tired and also hung over, bed seemed like the best place for me. John was so drunk, I had never seen him inebriated to that extent, and it was only after about an hour that I remembered there were many swimming pools John would have to pass on the way back to our hotel room.

I wanted to get up out of bed and check on him and make sure he was okay, but I was too tired. I quickly called on the angels to watch over him and fell asleep. At 3.30 in the morning, I was suddenly awoken by the repulsive sound of John vomiting in our hotel spa bath, and the stench was so disgusting that I had to open all the doors and windows. I still don't know how John found his way back to the apartment on his own in his drunken state—he told me that no one had helped him—without falling into some body of water. I silently thanked the angels and couldn't believe they also helped drunks.

On the fourth night, we were taken on tour for a wedding onboard a boat. My intuition was nagging me to take a coat, as it would get colder. John thought that it was very foolish of me to even bother, as the weather was so warm, and he told me not to bring anything. I wish I had listened to my intuition and not my partner. It was freezing cold on the cruise; that very night that I began coughing and I ended up having the flu for three weeks. Isn't romance just a beautiful thing. I let my boyfriend's ego get in the way of my own intuition. The things we do for love.

The dinners and the boat tours were all paid for by John's company and we were treated like royalty. When I did have time on my own, I would go and lie on one of the sundecks located just outside our hotel room. Fiji was a little slice of heaven.

On the trip back home, I was not convinced that John's trips to the hypnotherapist had fully worked. When he saw how big the plane was, he seemed to panic, and once onboard the aircraft, he couldn't sit still in his seat. The doctor had given him two little tablets of Valium, so he could take them if he felt that he couldn't relax. He prescribed them only as a last resort, if all the counseling and hypnotherapy had failed John.

John didn't even hesitate. As soon as the plane began to take off, he popped not one but both pills. I was also edgy, as I picked up on his anxiety, and I was not very happy with his constant moving around. I also had the beginnings of my menstrual cycle coming on, and I was feeling incredibly sharp pains in my upper legs. I didn't know how I was going to relax in my seat for the entire five-hour trip and I called on my angels for some major help. Of course, I also called on them to make certain that there would be less turbulence on the plane and to help keep us safe on the flight.

Getting off the plane, I was dizzy and tired. We headed off to collect our luggage. John seemed suddenly okay. It was almost like the plane trip never happened. He was smiling away and full of energy. I was still recovering and I was going to have to for the next three weeks.

John was a salesman for a major water company, and a very good one at that. What made John a fantastic salesman was not that he lied, it was actually that he told the truth. He loved his job and found it very easy to make top sales for his company, as he believed wholeheartedly in the product and therefore, clients trusted him. He sold water filters that were installed in sinks and the water supply was delicious, so I enjoyed drinking it, too.

His top sales enabled him to take advantage of some great incentives. John's nature as a very positive person manifested in his life in pleasant ways. He was a very good example to me, as I could still have my negative moments and he was able to show me that this was not necessary. It was strange that I had taught so many women to be more positive and to manifest positive outcomes in their lives, yet I could have my own moments of self-destructive behavior.

* * *

It seemed like I had focused for years on manifesting a new car, which I desperately needed. My car had become a death trap and I definitely felt unsafe driving it. It didn't have power-steering, either, so the steering wheel was incredibly difficult to use and my neck was beginning to hurt because of it. I was frustrated as I had been trying to manifest positive outcomes in my life for a while now, hoping for a better financial situation, but I wasn't yet seeing any results. I had given much of my life to healing others and I was certain that I was destined to be on this path, yet my body and mind were becoming burnt out. The angels still wanted me to help others but to do this I had to be financially secure.

For the majority of my life, I'd experienced negative issues with money. I never had enough money, and I always had trouble saving. Since I had been unwell for most of my life, it had been difficult to make any substantial amount. Money and I didn't seem to mix so well, and I needed to finally change my negative, unhealthy views on it. Whenever I tried to search for another job—let's call it a 'normal' job—my intuition has always stopped me. I had to trust that work would come my way in the form of more clientele. Thank God, it always has.

Until I had completely cleared and healed my negative beliefs about money, I would only be attracting more financial debts and financial problems. It was finally in 2009 that I began to see what other people had meant, that money could actually flow to me. It was then that I came to understand the power of manifestation.

Money is important in life and is very much a necessity. I don't believe in being greedy, but money is vital in allowing people to develop even more on the spiritual plane. It enables you not to stress when doing simple things such as buying groceries or paying house bills, and to travel and enjoy life. If we don't have things to look forward to in life, we can become depressed and bitter. I was finally on the path to manifesting things I really needed in my life, and one of them was a new car. John was the angel who was able to help manifest this for me. He offered to find it for me and to get it at a great price. I paid for it with my money, although John loaned me the money, as I was waiting on some funds to come through which took a couple of months.

My health was the reason for my hopeless financial situation and the reason I only worked part-time. Even though I had helped so many women, none of them were aware of my own health issues and that I had suffered severely with migraines for a large part of my life. I was healing myself while healing them, and I was certain that somehow the angels were making me stronger and better. It had no doubt been a difficult and lengthy process but I was determined to see the miracle of God and the angels heal me completely.

Affirmation: "I accept myself for the amazing person that I am. I approve of myself."

Copy the affirmation on the prior page as many times as you wish.

CHAPTER 12

Standing in my truth

I was booked in to see a male doctor. This time, I needed medical attention as I had been experiencing some slight asthma. I entered his room and sat down to speak to him. He looked into my asthma problem and after examining me, he said it was nothing major. He told me to keep an eye on it and use a puffer now and then.

He then proceeded to ask me what I was doing as an occupation. I told him that I was a natural healer. He then drilled me with questions, so I told him exactly what I was doing—working as a psychic. Well, I couldn't believe his response. He had the nerve to tell me that what I was doing was wrong, and I should leave my job immediately. I looked at him for quite some time and once I had composed myself, I spoke my mind. I told him that I was happy being a psychic and there was nothing wrong with what I was doing. I told him that he was being way too judgmental and unfair.

I immediately got up from my seat and stormed out of his room, and almost ran out of the medical center. I was so shocked at his blunt manner and was so offended by his behavior. I couldn't believe that I had just gone for a medical check-up and instead, my work had suddenly become the main focus of the session. It seemed that some people still believed that psychics were going to hell.

Affirmation: "I love life. Life has so many wonderful things to offer. I accept life's gifts with open arms."

Copy the affirmation on the prior page as many times as you wish.

CHAPTER 13

Respecting the beliefs of others

John and I were driving to a Greek Orthodox Church for his Easter celebration. He was giving me some instructions on how to drink the wine, and how I needed to light a candle and kiss two paintings of holy figures. He told me to just copy him and follow what he did and I would be okay. We waited patiently in the queue that seemed to be moving at a rapid pace.

As we entered the church, I watched him carefully and did exactly the same as John. After lighting the candle, I followed him towards the two priests. John whispered to me that they would speak to me in Greek and all I needed to say to them was my name. I was called over to an old-looking priest who appeared to have a very strict energy about him. He rambled on in his foreign language. I couldn't comprehend one word he was saying. I just nodded and said my name to him.

Thinking that he would then give me a sip of the holy wine, I leaned forward a little. Instead, he looked at me with confusion and spoke again in his foreign tongue. Now I was feeling confused, as I thought I just had to say my name and I could have some of the wine and bread and leave. I repeated my name once again, and he suddenly spoke in English and asked me if I was Greek Orthodox. When I replied 'No', he shook his head and said that I couldn't drink the wine.

John was desperate for me to have the holy wine, as he believed

87

it to be therapeutic for me and very healing in its own way. So, he had hoped I would just slip by the two priests and they would not notice I was from a different background. I guess his plan backfired; however, I fully respected the priest's wishes.

I looked around me. The tiny church, with its beautiful interior, was completely packed. We made our way out of the church, back to our car. John put his arms around me and pulled me close to him. I smiled to myself. He leaned in and gave me a kiss on the cheek. "Happy Easter, darling. This is our very first Easter together!" I silently prayed that there would be many more to come.

Back home later that night, I shut the door to our bedroom and left John to watch some television. I turned off the bedroom light and I lit a beautiful white candle that was sitting on my bedside table. Then I knelt before the candle and I closed my eyes, and I prayed.

* * *

How does a 'Catholic girl' become involved in talking to and praying to angels? I don't recall ever not believing in angels. I remember seeing them as a child, hovering over my bed and protecting me. I still pray to Jesus and Mother Mary. How can praying to an angel be considered a sin? I have never committed a serious crime, yet my belief in the healing power of angels could in some people's eyes be considered a horrible crime.

When I was younger, I was very much drawn to the peaceful energy of the church and I loved hearing stories about Jesus. When the priest would preach about being a 'good and caring person', I tried my best to do as he said. I still try my best. The only difference is that as I grew older, I came to realize that the Catholic religion was not the only one that existed. My small world was suddenly opened and I could see that no religion was right or wrong.

I do not wish to preach; that is not what my book is about. Each to their own. I am just explaining why I became drawn to angel energy, since this book is about my journey as a healer. When I pray, I pray to God and the angels. I don't just pray to angels. Maybe the angels are just some extra support for God. I feel as if God sometimes needs a little extra help with all the problems of the world. Maybe they are like big protective bodyguards surrounding God and helping Him with His duties in this world. God and the angels have helped to bring a smile back to my face and an incredible sense of peace. I can't help seeing large, beautiful angels. Yet if I had the choice, I wouldn't ever want to stop seeing them!

There is something so sacred about entering the doors of a church. There is something so holy about it. If you ever see me in a church, kneeling down with my eyes closed, just remember that I am praying, too, and I have every right to pray to God. Just because I see angels, doesn't mean I don't believe in the healing power of God. I also believe in the healing power of Jesus Christ and Mother Mary.

* * *

Sometimes I sense that Heaven is very close, like I can reach out and touch it. We can pass over at any moment and enter the next phase of our journey. I am not afraid to go to the other side; however, I don't feel ready yet, as I have more to do here on earth. Just look around, particularly at the news, and see how many people pass over in a day. It is inevitable and in my field of work, I am well aware of this concept. I find it sad, though, that we can be here on earth and then so suddenly, we have to leave everyone we love behind. As much as I believe in the other side, I still can't grasp the concept that we have to leave loved ones on the earth plane so suddenly.

I would be lying if I was to say that I accept death very easily.

Being a psychic, you would think that I would, especially when I believe so strongly in angels and the afterlife. It just isn't the case for me. I probably think of death even more, as I am confronted by it every day in my line of work. I guess you could say that I have a slight fear of it, as I know that I would miss everyone so dearly. Our time here on earth is so precious. I never take one day for granted, and neither do I take anyone in my life for granted.

The thought that myself or a loved one may pass over is upsetting to me and I want to spend as much time with them as possible. I fear that even though we will meet again in Heaven, I might have to wait a long time before I see them again. What if I don't have this kind of relationship with them ever again, just now, as it is, exactly as it is? Even though I am aware that Heaven definitely exists, I am still afraid to leave the people I love behind.

Each moment of our lives is so important and not to be wasted on negative energy, as it will never happen again. I know that I have to spend time with my loved ones in a positive way, no longer fighting or saying things that I may regret later on. Each moment in my life is as important as each breath I take. Time is valuable and I need to invest my positive energy into it, and simply love life and live it to the best of my ability.

When you hear stories that people are passing over to the other side at a young age, you get a wake-up call. If you close your eyes and pretend that nothing is happening and that you or your loved ones will not die until you're old and grey, then you sometimes go through life with no heart or passion at all. When you are aware that this could be your final moment here on earth and you may never see a loved one again, you begin to realize that you need to live life to the fullest. You must enjoy your time here and make the most of what you have. It's all going to pass so quickly. Before you know it, it will be your time to go. We all go sooner or later.

Affirmation: "I believe in love and romance."

Copy the affirmation on the prior page as many times as you wish.

CHAPTER 14

My sacred space

I often feel the need to retreat from the rest of the world and connect with God and the angels. It's healing and comforting to me, and it always helps to bring more harmony into my life. It brings clarity in certain situations and it confirms to me that I am doing okay in this world. I also try to get a good night's sleep if possible, except for weekends, when I go out and my head won't be hitting the pillow until late into the night. If I lack sleep, I tend to be moody and extremely sensitive the following day. When giving guidance to others, you need to be extremely awake and alert, or the accuracy and quality of the reading can be very poor. You also need to appear refreshed and awake out of respect for your clients. I discovered that I cannot do a reading for someone when I am tired, no matter how hard I try.

My deepest insights come to me while I am meditating or daydreaming, and these insights are crucial for my line of work. I often call on the angels to come into my dreams and clear up any issues that may cause difficulties. The following day, I feel better, and know the angels have intervened in my dreams to bring me more clarity with issues that seemed impossible to resolve.

The particular angel that I call on to help me sleep better is again the Archangel Raphael. Every time I have trouble falling asleep or there is too much noise and interference around me, I call on this angel and my sleep always ends up being deep and peaceful. This angel is connected to health and wellbeing, so I often send him to friends and family if they are unwell in any way.

Yoga is great for balancing the seven chakras and helps to promote great health and wellbeing. If the chakras are out of balance, chances are one's health will be, too. As a qualified reiki practitioner, I can help to balance the chakras and emotions. I practice reiki on myself on a regular basis, and I feel absolutely amazing after each personal reiki healing session. I perform reiki on some clients and the feedback has been reassuring that this relatively modern day practice, which is also being used in certain hospitals, is beneficial for people's health.

Exercise is essential for people, as it releases negative energy from the body. Walking is also a great form of exercise. Making time to exercise throughout the week is crucial for everyone, yet many people don't do any. They believe they don't have the time to exercise or the time to just be still, or to have fun with friends. It's all about manifesting time for enjoyment and relaxation.

I try to create the belief that I can have the time to do things I enjoy during the week. You can change the belief that you feel you don't have any time for yourself. You can manifest more peaceful time in your busy schedule. Suddenly you may find that you are able to have a little break from life's normal, busy routines.

Manifestation is all about the power of the mind and changing negative beliefs into positive outcomes. It simply takes some change in our thought patterns. We can allow the gates to magically open and suddenly, more sacred time is on the agenda. Speaking to a healer or holistic counselor, or even reading some great spiritual material, can assist someone to understand the topic of manifestation even further. Sometimes it takes time to comprehend this tool, as a person may have many traditional beliefs that need undoing, and a professional can help with this process. There are many women and men who are finally opening up to this concept, however, and wish to understand it more. Spiritual seminars also have some great information on manifestation.

One of the angels I work with frequently is Archangel Michael. Many healers tend to use him in their sessions. I call on him to help protect and relax the client. Another angel I work with is Archangel Raphael, whom I mentioned earlier. If a person is unwell, he helps to lift their energy vibration, simply by being sent to their side. The angels help with endless different issues, and all you need to do is to acknowledge their presence and have faith that they will be there, looking after your best interests.

It's very handy having the angels looking after me, and I remember to thank them and never take them for granted. It always feels like I have an angel around me somewhere, looking after me and bringing blessings my way. We all have our good days and bad days. The ability to see my angels allows me to pull myself out of my horrible moments. Just knowing that they are there, seeing them with my very own eyes, gives me hope and faith that things will be okay in the end.

* * *

I found that some people wanted to befriend me so that they could use me for my intuitive abilities. Let's say that these people wanted to have free readings and becoming my friend would make it easier for them to get psychic guidance free of charge. I was upset that they were trying to do this, and I had to be firm with them and tell them that I was not having any of that.

It's not that I didn't wish to help them with their problems, but I was beginning to realize that I was being taken for a fool. My abilities were not to be used for pure entertainment, either. I was not going to allow myself to become unwell in order to heal and help others. People had to pay for my services and see that I was not some hippie psychic who survived on pure fresh air. I had to make a living and I was not going to be Mother Teresa and save everyone while I lived in poverty. Many Empaths and healers in the past were taken advantage of and used for their services in the wrong manner. Many became extremely unwell and a lot of them died at a young age. I have seen some fall ill and burn out due to having helped too many souls, too often for free. I was not going to allow that to happen to me.

I recall one older beautiful, loving psychic who didn't listen to her boss at a healing center at which she worked when he told her not to allow clients to call her after hours so she could help them for free. I remember how he made it clear to her that she was becoming very stressed and ill, and that she needed a break from assisting too many people. He was not saying this because he wished to have them paying her after hours, it was because many of her clients were taking her for granted and she needed to be more respected as a psychic healer. Unfortunately, this lady didn't listen and she did become very ill—she had a breakdown. All those people she had helped were not going to give her any medal for her hard work and efforts, and they certainly were not going to hold her hand during her breakdown.

To help many people is not always such a holy deed, especially if it is going to make you unwell. God and the angels do not wish for you to heal others if you are going to become sick over it. Wisdom is not about healing the world, wisdom is about healing yourself and only helping others to the degree that you can handle.

People who feel that they always need to put others before themselves are usually doing this out of guilt or fear, and they can become very bitter and miserable. They find that all their energy goes out to their loved ones and they can become resentful, as they don't have any energy left for themselves. This is not a very smart way to live. Usually when you have more energy and time for yourself, you can then give even more easily to others.

Affirmation: "I am able to heal myself of any blocks that may be preventing me from finding my true love."

Copy the affirmation on the prior page as many times as you wish.

CHAPTER 15

Amore

There was one particular female client who came to see me at home and I kind of wish she hadn't. This woman was very well-dressed and attractive. Her background was Italian, from Sicily. Her hometown was sometimes known for murder and crime, and this part of Italy for its Mafia presence. Now, my grandmother on my mum's side was born in Sicily and she was definitely not hiding a gun under her bed, from what I have been told. No one in her family was hiding from the *polizia*. There were some good people in this little town but unfortunately, there were some bad ones, too.

The client who came to see me on that particular day was unfortunately connected to the 'bad' part, but her heart and soul wanted freedom from this way of life. It felt like a prison for her and she had never done anything like murder a person. She was trapped, as she had been brought up in one of the Mafia families and when you are born into such circumstances—well, you can imagine how difficult it was to get out.

I told her straight away that I couldn't answer any questions in regards to who had murdered who, as I didn't wish to get involved that way. In other words, to put it quite simply, I was terrified. I was not having any Mafia criminal come to my house and wait outside in the bushes to have me 'whacked'. No, thank you, I didn't need that kind of stress in my life. Instead, I helped guide her with her own personal love life and issues connected to travel and career. Those were much safer questions to answer.

Now I really liked this girl and I felt sorry for her, being amongst such sadness and madness. She suddenly told me that she didn't have enough money on her to make the payment. She informed me that she would transfer the funds into my account later that day. I wasn't going to mess with her, if you know what I mean. I tried to talk myself into believing that she would pay the money and it would be ok.

Unfortunately, two weeks passed and there was no sign of the money. So, I did what I thought I must do, I called her and hoped that maybe she had forgotten. She answered and I told her that I hadn't yet received the payment for my reading. She started to explain that as my attitude had changed once I had discovered that she was part of the Mafia, she didn't think I deserved it. I was confused, as I had only been nice to her.

Most rational people would have just agreed with her and hung up the phone, maybe even apologized for their own rude behavior, for even calling her. Not me, no—I started to tell her off and say that I was in the right and I deserved that money. Of course, she lost it at me, screaming down the phone, so finally, something clicked in me and I remembered who I was talking to. I calmed down and said that it was her decision what she should do, and I said goodbye. Then reality kicked in. Where had my mind gone? What the hell had I been thinking?

As you can imagine, for about a month after that, I didn't sleep at all and I constantly checked outside my window to see if there were any unwanted strangers. I even got John to change the television station if he was watching his favorite show, *The Sopranos*. Hell, I didn't need television: I was living the real thing. John seemed way too calm for my liking, as he sat on the couch, his eyes glued to the television set. He either thought that I was being extremely irrational or he was too scared himself to get involved in any way. Either way, he didn't seem the least bit affected by my anxiety attacks.

* * *

When you do this kind of work, you have to expect all kinds of clients and situations. Sometimes it is difficult to trust your intuition when you need to predict a very important outcome. In some cases, I can find it difficult to separate my heart from the circumstance, as I may really care about the person involved or the person asking the question. It can also seem like a great responsibility and I just don't want to get it wrong. However, when my emotions are involved, it can be difficult to always get it right. This is the very reason I no longer read for family or friends. I have had many of them ask me for a reading, and in the past I would feel pressured to help them out. I wanted to guide them with their issues or any difficulties they were experiencing. Yet, my accuracy was not the best, and my emotions and ego would get in the way. I already knew too much personal information about them, and that would cloud my reading considerably. I didn't believe it was wise to continue to guide them. Most therapists refuse to have family or friends as clients. A reading is similar to a counseling session, so it makes sense why I no longer run to the assistance of a relation or a close friend.

Women need to listen to their intuition more often. It is real. It does exist. Women who choose to ignore it tend to regret it later on, when it's too late. You can never turn back time, and if a major decision you made in your life has not been to your advantage, then you may recall ignoring your intuition, your gut instinct. Learning to listen to your inner truth—your inner voice—takes practice and courage. Listen to it, regardless of those who tell you otherwise, or that you are making the incorrect decision.

Your intuition becomes stronger through meditation, yoga, reiki and simply taking more time out for yourself, where you can reconnect with your soul. Having some alone time is important, so that you can block out the outside world and go within.

Affirmation: "I express myself in a clear and calm manner. I communicate with confidence."

Copy the affirmation on the prior page as many times as you wish.

CHAPTER 16

Cinderella and her intuition

The two women reminded me of the two ugly stepsisters from *Cinderella*. This nickname for these two women might appear harsh, but you might forgive me when you understand why I gave it to them.

I was attending their beauty salon for my monthly facial. I had booked in with one of the sisters, so she could help me keep my skin looking younger and healthier. Little did I know how inexperienced these two women were in their field. Given that they had been in the industry for over twenty years, I expected them to have had more knowledge in looking after their clients' skin.

I had been very pleased with their work the first three times I'd had a facial with them, so I was completely surprised when my fourth visit turned out to be something which I still consider a bit of a nightmare. I'd booked in for my usual half-hour facial and suddenly the sister who was working on me said in her thick Turkish accent, "Oh, I am not happy with your skin. No, this skin is not good at all. It is too oily! You have beautiful skin, but way too oily. That's okay. I fix it. You watch—I fix it like brand new. I also need to wax your eyebrows—they are too hairy." Her face hovered over mine as she examined my skin. *She should first think about waxing the hair on her upper lip and then worry about my eyebrows.*

"What do you mean?" I asked her. "How can you help get rid of the oil on my skin?" I was very puzzled by her statement and her observation about my skin, as it had never felt too oily. In fact, it could be a bit dry at times.

"Hilda will make it look like brand new skin and less oils. You have to trust me. I will do this fantastic new procedure on it and I will charge you a lot less. Just trust me. You have to trust Hilda."

Now, I don't know about you, but when an older lady with a thick European accent is trying to sell me something and tells me to 'trust them', I usually hear warning bells in my head. Before you accuse me of racism, please keep in mind that my background is half Italian and half Croatian. My father was born overseas in Croatia and arrived in Australia at the tender age of seventeen. He came on his own. His parents and his two sisters had remained back in Croatia. He had been very brave to venture overseas and start a new life for himself.

I was suddenly feeling very nauseated and I wanted to jump right off the massage bed. Whenever I don't listen to my intuition, my stomach starts to feel uneasy, since I am not listening to my 'gut instinct'. In this case, on this particular day at the beauty salon, my 'gut' didn't fully agree with this new facial procedure.

As Hilda's energy was very strong and persuasive—in other words, overbearingly pushy—I didn't stop her from going ahead with the 'new form of facial' she was talking about. Instead I gave in to her bossiness and I let her perform what I believe to this very day was a form of 'torture' on my face. My skin has always been extremely sensitive. Due to the migraines I suffered through my late teens and the majority of my twenties, harsh chemicals in facial products, hair products and body products have always been a big 'no-no' for me. So for many years, I have used products which contain fewer harsh chemicals and as a consequence my skin looks very young.

For this reason, I persisted with Hilda, explaining to her that my skin was too sensitive for the kind of treatment she wanted to carry out. Her accent was so powerful and her voice, so bossy, that I reluctantly gave in to her. My skin began stinging, even feeling pain as she sprayed what she insisted were natural oils onto my face. I wriggled and squirmed on the massage bed and it felt like I was at the dentist's getting my teeth pulled out. She kept saying to me, "Please, I know that you will absolutely thank me for doing this tomorrow when you look in the mirror. You will want to call me and say that I fixed your skin. It will look more beautiful than ever. Please trust Hilda."

Her sister strolled into the room and watched the procedure. At this point, I almost had tears in my eyes and was extremely stressed. My heart beat faster and I could barely breathe. *My poor face. What the hell is she doing to my face?* Then the thoughts changed to, *She's a professional. She knows what she's doing. The pain might be worth it once I have a good look at my face in the mirror.*

"Why, you lucky girl, Hilda knows what she is doing," her sister said in an even thicker accent. "You will be much pleased."

Unfortunately, I was anything but pleased. Hilda's chirpy voice suddenly changed to a more concerned tone. "That's enough. I stop now. You don't need more. Now your skin very red, but that will go away tomorrow when you wake up. I finish now."

I was so relieved to finally leave the torture bed and I silently prayed that my face would look okay when I looked in the mirror they had in the room. She had seemed to suddenly disappear, making a very quick exit from the room, leaving me to get my bag and coat. I looked in the mirror. When she'd said that my face looked a little red, she had somehow failed to mention that it resembled a ripe tomato. I was shocked to see how red it looked but I calmed down when I remembered her words that the redness would disappear in the morning.

Well, in the morning, my face was redder than ever. I called the doctor as soon as I awoke and made an appointment for the very next day. The female doctor inspected the skin on my face and said it looked irritated, and that there was nothing much I could do, except be very cautious what I put on my face. She believed it would eventually heal, but still was surprised that a facial treatment had caused my skin to react in such a way. Some improvement finally occurred after four weeks had passed. When the redness had finally disappeared, my skin was still not the same and I was in tears, as a girl knows the skin on her face.

Thank God my angels led me to a lady who worked at another beauty parlor, and she has since performed miracles on my skin. It now looks amazing. The moral of this story (again) is to always trust your intuition!

* * *

My acupuncturist believed that I had some kind of hormonal issue. I had to see her every two weeks, and she got me to lie flat on the table while she inserted little pins into me, and I usually fell asleep within twenty minutes of the procedure. Sometimes I could see angels in that room sending me their healing light, telling me that I would be okay.

Her words disturbed me, but I was also strangely calm. She explained to me that I may have difficulties in bearing children and that I may experience issues with being fertile. She believed that since my period was irregular and lasted too long, I may never have children. The words cut me like a knife, straight through my heart. Tears welled up in my eyes. I thought of my husband John and of how much he longed to have children. Then a strange calm overcame me. That peaceful feeling stayed within me; it didn't leave even as she rambled on about this painful prospect of never having a little angel to mother.

A beautiful emerald green light surrounded me in the room of this tiny acupuncture medical center. Archangel Raphael was hovering above me as the acupuncturist continued to speak. The angel known for his tremendous ability to heal. He told me that I needed some medical attention, and to have some herbal medicine and I would heal. Everything would be okay. I could hear him gently whispering to me to allow destiny to take this matter into her hands. This was not for me to control. If I was meant to fall pregnant, then nothing would stop me. If I was not meant to have children, then I would learn to embrace acceptance.

I started to focus once again on my healer, who was standing next to the bed. As she lit a candle and turned off the light to leave me be, I fell into a deep sleep and I dreamed the sweetest dreams.

I would need to have blood tests and an ultrasound, just to determine that there was nothing medically wrong with me. I would have to do what my medical practitioner asked of me and what was expected of a client when they had issues with their menstrual cycle. I would have to go through with the 'procedures', but all the while, my thoughts would center around the fact that in the end, I would be fine. I wouldn't let the disturbed or confused expressions of the medical practitioners examining me upset me. I wouldn't allow the 'examinations' to get me into a state of extreme panic, thinking that I might not bear children one day. Instead, I would recall the vision I had of Archangel Raphael hovering above me in the little acupuncture room.

Affirmation: "I create healthy boundaries in my life. I move on from those that have tried to bring me down."

Copy the affirmation on the prior page as many times as you wish.

CHAPTER 17

Walk beside me

My life has in no way been perfect and I am definitely not insinuating that I, myself, have been perfect. There have been times in my life when I haven't acted in the most 'angelic' way, or even close to that. There are times in my past that I don't wish to remember and I am not proud of at all. Please don't ever assume that my moods have always been calm and relaxed. It's just that reconnecting with my inner spirit and having the knowledge that the angels and God still love me regardless of anything else, now makes it easier when something really aggravates me.

Just because I read angel cards and have the ability to see the angels, doesn't mean that I am constantly helping others—that I am always donating to third world countries, praying on my knees for world peace, helping little old ladies to cross the road, meditating twenty-four hours a day, and constantly on my best behavior. I am only human, and I express my all-too-human hurt at times. Whether it comes across as angelic, I highly doubt it.

I went through a stage in my life in which I felt completely disrespected and lied to by many people. To say that I was fine about it all and that none of it affected me in any way would not be the slightest bit true. It made me angry, and on occasions, I completely lost my cool.

So, I might be able to see angels but I, like most people, am no angel myself. I have had my moments in the past and I might in the years to come. Being a healer, however, makes me wiser and I have learnt that having peace and harmony in relationships is definitely possible. Having harmony in my own life has also come about, due to my spiritual path.

* * *

Sometimes people come into our lives to teach us very important things. They have a huge impact on us and we can never forget them. I have often felt that we are all on a journey to heal ourselves and we are also on a journey to heal those we love.

One woman who entered my life was called 'Melissa'. She was a very strong and centered lady, with a heart of gold. Her wisdom was tremendous and her knowledge was very healing. She came into my life as a teacher, to help me get through the lonely and painful period of my life. Her life had also had its ups and downs, but her willpower and her happiness, regardless of what she had endured, was something that I really admired. We've likely all had a mentor at some time in our lives, someone we looked up to and who gave us inspiration and courage. Melissa has been my mentor through the years and I will always thank her for her ability to help keep me on the right path.

My mother is another mentor of mine. Her wisdom and her strength is something that has been instilled in me over the years. Her love for me has been so strong that it has been able to see me through the most difficult times of my life. I can't even begin to explain how she has been able to assist me over the years, and her own intuition, whether she's aware of it or not, comes through at just the right moment. I am certain that it hasn't been easy for her to have a daughter who chose to work as a psychic. I am fully aware how it tore her in two, due to her strong Catholic background. Her love for me is so strong, however, that she still holds my hand, even when she is conflicted. She still loves me just the same, and as long as I live, I will never forget her ability to do that for me.

We all need people who we can call on for help and advice, when the going gets tough. We all need someone to tell us that we are going to be okay, someone to enable us to continue on our paths and guide us in the right direction. We make up our own minds in the end: we have the willpower to do this and it is our divine right that no one can interfere with our final choices. Yet there's something about the strength and faith within us that seems to become even stronger as soon as a wise and caring person tells us that we are going to be okay. When they give their advice and guidance, they are doing it simply because they love us. It's like an angel hovering above us, guiding us and showing us the way.

* * *

My parents visited a psychic when I was around the age of twenty. I had no idea about this secret visit of theirs and it surprised me considerably when I found out. My parents are quite traditional and it is not something I would ever have imagined them doing.

My mum pulled me aside a couple of days after their session with the psychic, and she told me they were asked to bring photos of their children. She rambled on about how the psychic had spoken of me frequently and had told both of them that I was very gifted and would help many people. They were both shocked by this prediction, as my abilities were still suppressed at this point in my life. They knew nothing of my psychic gifts, as I had not yet accepted them or fully understood them.

My parents had gone to see this lady to see if she could foretell other things such as money prospects, and purely out of curiosity. They never imagined that the main focus of the session would be predictions of their own daughter becoming similar to the very lady who was sitting opposite them, laying out a deck of cards on the table and demonstrating her gift for foretelling their future.

I was not really shocked by this piece of news, the day my mother pulled me aside, yet I was still a little taken aback by this lady's deep insight. She had somehow got some vibes about me from the photo that my parents had presented to her. She had never met me and I had never met her, yet she relayed this piece of information to my parents, which they passed on to me.

This was just the kind of news I needed to hear, since I had recently been struggling with the concept of accepting my gifts. This psychic confirmed to me that this was the exact direction in which I should be headed, and that later on in my life, even though I was unaware at the time, it would become my chosen career.

Affirmation: "I am very gentle with myself. I am kind and loving towards myself."

Copy the affirmation on the prior page as many times as you wish.

CHAPTER 18

There you are

Sometimes I feel like a secret detective, hiding my true identity from so many people. Only those that wish to have readings and are open minded and spiritual, know the real me and what I do for a living. The rest of humanity is completely unaware of my real occupation, and there are unfortunately those who are also in denial. Yes, they are the people in my life who pretend that I am exactly like them, and that I don't do that psychic thing that I shouldn't be doing. So, I either do not bring it up in my conversations with them, or I simply pretend to be someone I am not for those one or two hours I am in their company. Then when I leave them, I enter my home, my sacred space and I am completely free to be me, whether that means I watch television, read a book, or listen to some music. The crystals, the angel oracle cards are not always out for display and my enjoyment. I am not always burning candles or meditating like a monk on a mountain hilltop. I am also not constantly helping clients or friends with my insights. There is balance in my life and I love it that way. Yet, when I am in the company of those who do not and never will understand my lifestyle or my beliefs, I find it easier to just pretend. I may not be the best actress, but for me, this is what I feel I need to do, for sometimes it's easier to pretend, rather than explain to those who just don't get me.

* * *

The power of the angels can be summed up in one particular outing we had with a couple we knew and their children. We were all hanging out at a popular pizza place, just enjoying the night. The parents' young daughter was completely engrossed in her own artwork, her mind solely focused on drawing two beautiful-looking fairies. She was so lost in her work that she didn't even want to have one bite of her pizza, which was sitting there beside her on the table, growing cold.

Just two days earlier, I had been rummaging through some of my paperwork, which I had neglected for quite some time, and I had come across an angel oracle card, lost amongst this pile of work. The angel featured on this card was the Archangel Ariel. I smiled to myself, happy to have found this card, as I had completely forgotten about the wonderful abilities of this particular angel. Archangel Ariel was able to assist those who called upon her to manifest great things in their lives.

Now, I was surprised to see that this adorable little girl bringing these two little fairies to life had given them each a name. In her neat little handwriting, she had carefully placed the name 'Sandy' above one of them. Then, to my delight and surprise, I noticed that she had called the other one 'Ariel'. I asked her why she had called the second fairy 'Ariel'. She just looked at me and shrugged her shoulders and said, "I don't know why. I just liked the name."

Angels can give certain signs that they are around you. Ariel was trying to show me that she was watching over me, through the sudden discovery of my oracle card and through the little girl's drawing of the fairy.

* * *

It was very late one cold winter's night back in Melbourne when John and I were walking after leaving a party in the city.

Our car seemed to be parked a mile away and I tried to get closer to him for some warmth.

There had been moments in my life when I could become withdrawn, due to the fact that some people didn't accept my abilities. It would sometimes cause me sadness. I have always been very sensitive.

John put things into perspective for me. On this windy night, he was able to bring some light to the situation. It seemed that my insecurities had got the better of me. John explained to me how much his friends really liked me and had told him how nice they all thought I was. On this occasion, it seemed I had misjudged what people thought of me.

If I allowed myself to be concerned with what others were thinking about me, it would definitely lower my energy and affect me and even my health. I knew that I mustn't worry about what others believed of me; I had to hold my head high.

Some people don't realize that psychics are just like everyone else. The only difference is that we are here to teach others about the afterlife. People forget or don't understand that we lead very normal lives. Having fun with friends, going to the movies, having coffee and hanging out with family is all very much on my agenda. Doing things that are enjoyable is a priority for me. Balancing my life is very important. Lucky for me, I have some beautiful, caring friends that support my work and my beliefs in every way. It makes a huge difference when there are some people around you, who fully accept you as you are.

Coming out of the closet as a psychic was not an easy thing for me. I could have stayed hidden there for ages, maybe even forever. Sometimes it's easier to hide from the rest of the world. I finally chose not to: I chose to come out of the closet and share my gifts. Many others have come out, too, and I am certain that there will be more.

If I really need to thank someone for their complete acceptance of me and my abilities, it would have to be John. He has understood me. He also sees the feedback from my clients, who thank me through written testimonials or by phone. Some clients want privacy, so they prefer to email me positive feedback. Being an Empath is so natural to me that I can't even contemplate doing something else for work. It's as natural as the air I breathe. I often say to John that I feel more 'normal' doing this for a living than any other form of employment. This is who I am and I do not apologize for my gifts. They are called gifts for a reason, and I intend to hold my head up high for I am so fortunate to have them.

John is able to give me knowledge that I would not get from any book or spiritual healer. He has advice for me that is so important in life, and that's why my angels made me wait for him. I also believe he has become stronger and happier with me in his life. Of course, we have had to work through issues and overcome obstacles,but I believe it has all been worth it in the end.

I always knew that when the time was right, my angels would send me someone who would love me unconditionally. If we had met earlier, as John often wishes, I believe that the timing would have been wrong and the relationship would not have endured. We both still had things to experience and people we were destined to meet along the way. We were not ready for full commitment to each other back then.

So, you see, my angels were always watching over me, and never once did they leave my side. They were there every step of the way, hearing my prayers to 'meet the man of my dreams'. They were there guiding me, reassuring me that he was already there, even when I was dating all of the other men. They knew I was going to be okay. They could see him already. It just hadn't been my time. I had other men to meet first, other men to experience and other men to kiss—other men's hearts to break, and my own heart had to be broken, too.

Yet I always had faith that the angels were protecting me and had my best interests at heart. I was always aware that someone special would walk into my life at just the right time.

* * *

There he is, standing over by the restaurant. He has his sunglasses in one hand and he is waiting for me. I feel like I have known him forever. He's not just another date. He smiles at me and again, I recognize that smile. He guides us both into the restaurant and beckons the waiter over. We have dinner together. He understands me without me having to say one word. I go home with him and I sleep in our bed together, and I can awake in the morning beside him. He was definitely worth the wait!

Epilogue

John and I got married in a Greek Orthodox Church. We travelled around Europe for our honeymoon, but not without some Rescue Remedy spray. My daughter was born one year later. Her smiles and laughter fill me with tremendous joy. Life goes on.

Affirmation: "I forgive myself. I learn from my past mistakes. I am allowed to make mistakes."

Copy the affirmation on the prior page as many times as you wish.

Acknowledgements

I wish to thank my supportive and caring friends, Effie Kargakis, Dorothy Bramich, Carmille Bawden, Maria Constantinou Highfield, Fiona Low, Sonia Petruccelli and Julie D'Ambrosio. Without your constant advice, wisdom and positive belief in me, I would never have had the courage to manifest and produce this memoir. My past includes all of you and I know deep in my heart, my future does too. I also wish to acknowledge Hiromi Mitsuya for her support and advice. I am grateful for my editor Serena Sandrin. Your wisdom and kindness has been invaluable. I also want to thank my husband, John, for all his encouragement. Thank you for supporting me in so many countless ways.

Notes